THE

DIVINE ECONOMICS

OF

MONEY

15 Timeless Money Management Lessons from the Bible for your Financial Success

Melissa Daniels

TABLE OF CONTENTS

INTRODUCTION

Have you ever experienced a moment that completely altered the course of your life? A moment so profound, it lingered in your thoughts and eventually led you down a new path? For me, that moment came when I stumbled upon a powerful verse in the Bible that forever changed my perspective on money and wealth.

Allow me to whisk you away on a transformative journey where ancient wisdom meets modern financial prowess in "The Divine Economics of Money: 15 Timeless Money Management Lessons from the Bible for your Financial Success." Within the pages of this book, I've meticulously curated a collection of invaluable insights gleaned from sacred scriptures to guide you towards financial abundance, peace, and purpose.

As we navigate the turbulent waters of personal finance together, it's crucial to acknowledge the common struggles that often plague us in our quest for financial well-being. Debt looms like a shadow, carrying the weight of stress and uncertainty, while society's relentless pursuit of material wealth can cloud our judgment and foster discontentment. In the midst of these challenges, the teachings of the Bible offer a beacon of hope, providing us with timeless principles on wise management, generosity, and contentment that are as relevant today as they were in the past centuries.

What sets this book apart is its unwavering commitment to equipping you with practical and actionable tips derived from the pages of the Bible. Each of the 15 insights shared within these chapters is a stepping stone towards financial peace and purpose, designed to inspire and empower you on your unique financial journey.

My personal journey into writing this book was sparked by a profound moment of clarity and revelation. Several years ago, I found myself entangled in a web of financial woes, my mind consumed by worries about bills, debts, and an uncertain future. It was during this dark period that I turned to the Bible for solace and guidance. As I delved deeper into its teachings, I discovered a wealth of wisdom that not only alleviated my financial burdens but also reshaped my entire outlook on money and wealth.

The turning point came when I stumbled upon a verse that spoke directly to my struggles, offering a simple yet profound truth that illuminated my path forward. It was at that moment of divine revelation that the idea for this book was born—a desire to share the transformative power of biblical wisdom with others who, like me, were seeking a way out of financial turmoil and into a life of abundance and purpose.

So, dear reader, I invite you to embark on this journey with me. Let the pages of this book be your guide, your companion, and your source of inspiration as you navigate the complex terrain of money and faith even if you are not a Bible believer. Together, let us unlock the secrets of divine money and chart a course towards financial freedom and fulfillment.

Take this first step today. Dive into the pages that follow, absorb the wisdom they contain, and let the timeless principles of the ancient book illuminate your path to a brighter financial future. Your journey begins now.

Chapter 1

Unveiling Your Treasure Map: Understanding Assets and Liabilities

"Be diligent to know the state of your flocks, and pay attention to your herds."
-Proverbs 27:23 (AMP)

Remember that dusty attic from your childhood, overflowing with forgotten toys, half-read books, and maybe even a treasure chest you imagined held untold riches? Picture yourself sifting through those items, separating the truly valuable from the clutter. That's precisely what we're going to do in this chapter, but instead of an attic, it's your financial landscape we'll explore. Get ready to embark on a journey of self-discovery, unearthing hidden gems and acknowledging the things that might be holding you back.

My own journey with understanding assets and liabilities wasn't always smooth sailing. Like many, I started out navigating my finances on autopilot, fueled by a mix of hope and naivety. I landed my first job after college, thrilled with the independence and the newfound ability to "buy things." Soon, credit cards became my companions, whispering promises of instant gratification. Fast forward a few years, and amidst the accumulating "stuff," I felt a creeping anxiety. Where had all the money gone? Was I ever going to achieve the financial security I craved? I was navigating through the complexities of managing finances, relationships, and responsibilities, seeking a balance that seemed elusive.

It was a verse from Proverbs 27:23 (NKJV) that became my wake-up call: "Be diligent to know the state of your flocks, and pay attention to your herds." This wasn't just about livestock; it was a nudge to take ownership of my financial situation. Just like a shepherd needs to examine the health of their flock, I needed to assess my financial well-being. So, I embarked on a financial audit, digging deeper into my expenses and income. What I discovered was a harsh reality: the credit card debt, the impulsive purchases, they were all liabilities, draining my resources like leaky faucets. On the other hand, my skills, education, and even my positive attitude emerged as assets, potential strengths to leverage for a brighter future.

This exercise, inspired by God's call to stewardship, became the turning point. It wasn't about feeling shame or defeat; it was about gaining clarity and empowerment. Just like the parable of the talents (Matthew 25:14-30), where the master entrusts his servants with resources, I realized I had been given valuable assets, both tangible and intangible. The key was to identify, nurture, and utilize them wisely.

Assets, in the conventional sense, are equated with material wealth and possessions—houses, cars, investments. Imagine your financial situation as a balance sheet, similar to the one businesses use. On one side, you have your assets, then your liabilities on the other side. Your assets represent anything that holds value and generates income or future benefits. Think of your savings, investments, retirement accounts, even your education and skills. They're your treasure chest, filled with potential.

While these are important, true assets extend beyond the tangible to include qualities that enrich our lives and the lives of those around us.

Reflecting on this, I realized that our assets are not solely defined by our bank accounts or possessions but also by the virtues and talents bestowed upon us. Kindness, compassion, wisdom, creativity—these are invaluable assets that enrich our existence and enable us to positively impact the world around us.

Conversely, liabilities are often viewed negatively as burdens, debts, loans, hindrances and anything that drains your resources. Credit card balances, unpaid bills, even subscriptions you rarely use fall into this category. These are the items taking up space in your attic, offering no real value and potentially hindering your progress.. They weigh us down, limiting our potential and hindering our growth. Psalm 38:4 (NKJV) poignantly captures this sentiment, "For my iniquities have gone over my head; like a heavy burden, they are too heavy for me." Liabilities can manifest in various forms—unresolved conflicts, unhealthy habits, toxic relationships—that drain our energy and erode our well-being.

Here's the real magic: knowing your assets and liabilities empowers you to make informed decisions. Think of it as financial literacy, similar to the Proverbs 4:7 (NASB) "The beginning of wisdom is: Acquire wisdom; And with all your possessions, acquire understanding." Just like acquiring knowledge empowers you in life, understanding your financial standing empowers you to make choices that align with your goals.

In today's fast-paced world, it can be easy to lose sight of our assets amidst the demands and distractions that surround us. The lure of material possessions, societal expectations, and comparison with others can obscure the true essence of what comprises our assets. Cautioning us is Matthew 16:26 (NIV)"What good will it be for someone to gain the whole world, yet forfeit their soul? Or what can anyone give in exchange for their soul?"

As individuals navigating the complexities in a season like this, it is vital to discern between fleeting possessions and enduring assets.

Exploring real-life examples of assets reveals the significance they hold in various aspects of our lives. For instance, a savings account acts as a safety net, akin to a hidden gem in one's treasure chest. Investments like stocks, bonds, and mutual funds represent opportunities for future growth, much like planting seeds in fertile ground. Retirement accounts are tailored investments aimed at securing a comfortable future during one's golden years.

Moreover, education and skills are assets of immense value, akin to the tools a skilled craftsman wields. In the same vein, strong relationships serve as invaluable assets, offering both emotional and at times, financial support. Investing in meaningful relationships cultivates a support system that sustains us through life's trials and triumphs, enriching our journey immeasurably.

Taking **Time** as an exemplary asset, it stands out as a precious resource that once spent, cannot be reclaimed. Our investment of time serves as a reflection of our values and priorities. Ephesians 5:15-16 urges us to continue to be vigilant in the way we conduct ourselves, choosing wisdom over folly and maximizing our use of time, recognizing that evil pervades each day. This passage underscores the importance of being mindful of how we utilize our time and advocating for wise decisions to make the most of it as the days are fleeting.

Liabilities encompass various aspects that can impact your financial stability. High-interest credit card debt acts like a relentless force draining your financial resources. Overdue bills continue to accrue interest silently, compounding and accumulating causing financial strain and depleting your hard-earned income.

Unused subscriptions represent recurring expenses for services seldom utilized, akin to unwanted clutter accumulating in your attic. High-interest personal loans can swiftly snowball into a substantial burden if not managed properly.

Additionally, negative self-talk, resembling a defeatist mindset, can impede your financial advancement, much like a broken compass misguiding your path.

Proverbs 22:24-25 (ESV) also warns against entangling ourselves with negative influences, "Make no friendship with a man given to anger, nor go with a wrathful man, lest you learn his ways and entangle yourself in a snare."

Remember, this isn't about shame or judgment. It's about awareness and empowerment. Just like the parable of the lost sheep (Luke 15:3-7), where the shepherd tirelessly searches for the lost one, your goal is to identify and address any "lost sheep" in your financial landscape. Perhaps you have a forgotten bank account with dormant funds, or maybe untapped skills that could be generating income through freelancing or side hustles. The key is to be proactive and explore all possibilities.

As you embark on this journey of self-discovery, remember this powerful verse from Proverbs 13:23 (KJV) "Much food is in the tillage of the poor, but there is that which is destroyed for want of judgment." Just like tilling the land reveals its potential bounty, examining your finances illuminates growth opportunities.

Here are a few tangible actions to help you begin:
Gather your documents: Collect bank statements, credit card bills, investment reports, and anything else that reflects your financial picture.

Create a list: Divide a sheet of paper into two columns: Assets and Liabilities. List everything that fits under each category, no matter how big or small.

Value your Assets: Estimate the current value of your savings, investments, and possessions. Consider the income-generating potential of your skills and education.

Quantify your Liabilities: Calculate your total debt, including interest rates and monthly payments.

Factor in recurring expenses like subscriptions you rarely use.

Analyze your Balance sheet: Take a step back and compare your assets and liabilities. What does this tell you about your overall financial health? Are there areas where you can optimize your resources?

Remember, this isn't a one-time exercise. Regularly revisiting your assets and liabilities allows you to track progress, celebrate wins, and adjust your strategies as needed. Think of it as a continuous treasure hunt, uncovering new possibilities and refining your financial navigation skills over time.

Here's where the true joy of understanding your assets and liabilities lies. It's not just about numbers on a page; it's about gaining control, making informed choices, and aligning your finances with your values and goals. It's about creating a sense of security and freedom, similar to the peace of mind described in Philippians 4:6: that we should not be anxious about anything, but in everything by prayer and supplication with thanksgiving, we should allow our requests to be made known to God.

With a clear understanding of your financial landscape, you can approach the future with confidence and optimism, knowing that you have the tools and knowledge to navigate any challenge.

Embark on this adventure of self-discovery with an open mind and a hopeful heart. Remember, your financial potential is like a buried treasure waiting to be unearthed. By understanding your assets and liabilities, you are equipping yourself with the map and tools to unlock its true value and build a brighter financial future, one step at a time.

Chapter 2

Prioritize Giving: Cultivating a generous heart in Money management

"One person gives freely, yet gains even more; another withholds unduly, but comes to poverty."
-Proverbs 11:24-25 (NIV)

Have you for once experienced the joy that comes from giving freely, without expectation of return? Perhaps you witnessed a stranger in need and offered a helping hand, or maybe you contributed to a cause close to your heart. Did you notice a sense of inner satisfaction, a lightness In your step, or even a curious twist of fate that brought unexpected blessings your way? If so, you've tapped into the transformative power of generosity, a cornerstone of both spiritual and financial well-being.

The idea of giving might seem counterintuitive when it comes to managing money. After all, shouldn't we be focusing on acquiring and safeguarding our resources? Yet, countless verses throughout the Bible paint a different picture. As I navigated through my financial challenges, I found solace and direction in scriptures like Proverbs 11:24-25, which highlights the concept that "One person gives freely, yet gains even more; another withholds unduly, but comes to poverty." Similarly, Luke 6:38 (GNT) promises, "Give to others, and God will give to you. Indeed, you will receive a full measure, a generous helping, poured into your hands--all that you can hold. The measure you use for others is the one that God will use for you." These verses, and countless others, illuminate a fundamental truth: not a depletion of resources, but a powerful catalyst for abundance not just in material wealth but also spiritual fulfillment.

These verses challenged my perception of giving as a "loss." Could it be an invitation to abundance, a way to tap into a divine flow of blessings? So, I embarked on a mini-experiment. I set aside a small portion of my income for charitable donations, volunteering at a local soup kitchen amidst my busy schedule. The experience was transformative. Witnessing the smiles on grateful faces, the tangible impact of my contribution, sparked an unexpected joy, a sense of purpose I hadn't felt before. It wasn't just about the "giving," it was about connecting, serving, and being part of something bigger than myself.

Remember the parable of the talents (Matthew 25:14-30)? The master entrusts his servants with resources, expecting them to use them wisely, to grow them. We, too, are entrusted with resources, not just for personal gain, but also to contribute to the good of others. Prioritizing giving, even amidst limitations, aligns with this divine principle, allowing us to become active participants in a wider story of generosity and abundance.

It's natural to have concerns or objections when it comes to giving. Perhaps you feel like you don't have enough money to spare or worry that giving will leave you without a safety net. These fears are valid, but they shouldn't hold you back from embracing generosity.

Now, let's address a common misconception: generosity isn't synonymous with wastefulness. When you invest in fertile soil, quality seeds, and proper care for your garden, you expect a bountiful harvest, not wasted resources. Similarly, thoughtful giving, done with intention and research, ensures your contributions make a genuine impact. Supporting organizations with proven track records, volunteering your time strategically, or even choosing ethical businesses that reinvest in their communities are all ways to ensure your generosity truly blossoms.

Remember that giving doesn't have to be extravagant to make a difference. Every act of giving, big or small, has the potential to create ripples of positive change. It could be a kind word to a stranger, a donation to a local food bank, or simply choosing a sustainable product over a cheaper, less ethical alternative. Every action, fueled by a generous heart, contributes to a world where resources are shared more equitably, where kindness prevails, and where everyone has the opportunity to thrive

Incorporating generosity into your wealth management strategy doesn't have to be complicated. Simply imagine your financial resources as a fertile field, capable of producing not just for yourself, but for others as well. Planting seeds of generosity, through various avenues, can yield a bountiful harvest. Here are some practical tips from the holy book:

Set a Giving Goal: Just as you set financial goals for savings and investments, establish a giving goal based on a percentage of your income. Remember the words from 2 Corinthians 9:7 (NIV) "Each of you should give what you have decided in your heart to give, not reluctantly or under compulsion, for God loves a cheerful giver."

Embrace the Blessing of Tithing: Tithing, giving a tenth of your income, is a biblical principle mentioned in Malachi 3:10, where God promises to bless those who bring the whole tithe into the storehouse. Trust in this divine promise and experience the blessings that flow from faithful giving.

Expand Your Giving Circle: Look beyond monetary donations and explore other ways to give. Volunteer your time, skills, or talents to organizations in need. Participate in community service projects or initiatives that support a cause close to your heart. Remember, generosity isn't limited by financial resources; giving your time and energy holds immense value. As Proverbs 11:25 (NIV) states, "A generous person will prosper; whoever refreshes others will be refreshed."

Get Creative: Even with limited resources, you can find ways to be generous. Offer discounts or pro bono services to those in need, organize fundraising events within your community, or share your skills and knowledge through workshops or webinars. Remember, intention and thoughtfulness matter more than the size of the contribution. As Ecclesiastes 11:1 (NIV) reminds us, "Cast your bread upon the waters, for you will find it after many days." Even a small act of generosity, like a kind word or a helping hand, can have a ripple effect, creating positive change.

Seek Wise Counsel: Surround yourself with mentors or financial advisors who share your values regarding generosity. Proverbs 15:22 (NIV) reminds us, "Plans fail for lack of counsel, but with many advisers, they succeed." Seek guidance on how to give effectively and make a positive impact with your resources.

Address the Objections: It's natural to have concerns about giving, especially when finances feel tight. "What if I need the money later?" or "I don't have enough left over after bills and expenses" are common worries. Yet, consider this: countless testimonies demonstrate that when we prioritize giving, even amidst limitations, God often shows up in unexpected ways, providing for our needs and opening doors to abundance. Remember, faith and generosity go hand in hand.

As you continue on your path towards financial well-being, remember that generosity is not just a one-time gesture but a way of life. Cultivate a spirit of giving that extends beyond your financial transactions and permeates every aspect of your existence. By practicing generosity consistently and intentionally, you create a ripple effect of positivity and abundance that reverberates throughout the universe.

Embracing generosity in your financial journey isn't just about fulfilling an obligation; it's about aligning your actions with your values, experiencing the joy of service, and connecting with a higher and divine purpose. As Mahatma Gandhi beautifully said, "The best way to find yourself is to lose yourself in the service of others." By opening our hearts and hands to giving, we discover the true wealth that lies not in material possessions, but in the richness of connection, purpose, and a life infused with meaning.

Proverbs 19:17 has also declared that "Whoever is kind to the poor lends to the Lord, and he will reward them for what they have done." May your journey be filled with blessings, both given and received!

Chapter 3

Avoid Debt: Live within your means

"The rich rules over the poor, and the borrower is a slave to the lender."
– Proverbs 22:7 (ESV)

Remember the feeling of weightlessness you experience after scaling a mountain, reaching the summit and basking in the breathtaking view? Imagine achieving that same lightness, not after a physical climb, but by conquering a financial challenge: living debt-free within your means. Sounds impossible? Trust me, it's within reach, and just like any worthwhile expedition, requires preparation, determination, and a little divine guidance.

It is imperative that we explore the wisdom found in the scriptures to guide us in making crucial decisions.
Many have navigated the treacherous terrain of debt. The allure of instant gratification, the pressure to keep up with the Joneses, or simply unforeseen circumstances can easily land us in its slippery grip.

Debt can become a heavy chain, weighing down our spirits and limiting our choices.

In Proverbs 22:7 (ESV), it is written, "The rich rules over the poor, and the borrower is the slave of the lender." This powerful verse reminds us of the potential consequences of falling into the trap of debt. Debt can enslave us, limiting our freedom and causing undue stress. We are encouraged to be wise stewards of our finances, making decisions that align with our values and long-term goals.

Imagine a young couple, Sarah and John, who decided to upgrade to a larger house beyond their budget, convinced that they could manage the higher mortgage payments. Initially, they were filled with excitement and anticipation. However, as unexpected expenses arose and interest rates increased, they found themselves drowning in debt, unable to meet their financial obligations. The burden of debt strained their marriage and overshadowed their joy, highlighting the importance of financial prudence.

Living within your means does not mean living a life devoid of joy or comfort. It means making intentional choices that align with your values and priorities. They are timeless principles that have stood the test of time, echoed throughout the pages of the Bible.

Consider Hannah, a single mother balancing work and family responsibilities. Despite her modest income, she found creative ways to enjoy life without accumulating debt. She cultivated a garden, cooked nourishing meals at home, and engaged in free community activities with her children. By prioritizing experiences over material possessions, she built a life filled with richness and contentment.

One of the key principles that the Bible emphasizes is the idea of contentment. In Philippians 4:11-13, the apostle Paul writes, "I have learned to be content whatever the circumstances. I know what it is to be In need, and I know what it is to have plenty." Contentment enables us to cherish the things we already have and prevents us from succumbing to the desire to go into debt in order to acquire more material possessions. It is a mindset that fosters gratitude and happiness, irrespective of our circumstances.

The Bible also teaches us the importance of planning and diligence in managing our finances. In Proverbs 21:5 (ESV), it is written, "The plans of the diligent lead surely to abundance, but everyone who is hasty comes only to poverty." Planning involves setting financial goals, creating a budget, and making informed decisions about spending and saving. It requires discipline and diligence to stay on course, even when faced with temptations or unexpected challenges.

Reflecting on the story of Joseph in the Book of Genesis. Through his foresight and prudent management of resources during times of abundance, he was able to save Egypt from famine and ensure the well-being of his family. Joseph's example demonstrates the profound impact of wise financial planning and stewardship. By being intentional with our finances, we can secure our future and navigate uncertainties with confidence.

In the fast-paced world of the 21st century, we are bombarded with messages that promote instant gratification and consumerism. The allure of credit cards, loans, and buy-now-pay-later schemes can lead us astray, tempting us to live beyond our means. However, the Bible offers us a different perspective, urging us to exercise self-control and prudence in all aspects of life, including finances.

Consider the parable of the talents in Matthew 25:14-30, where Jesus illustrates the importance of stewardship and accountability. The servants who invested their talents wisely were commended and entrusted with greater responsibilities, while the one who buried his talent out of fear faced consequences. This parable reminds us of the need to make the most of our resources, using them wisely and responsibly for the benefit of ourselves and others. Embarking on this liberating journey involves several key steps. The first step is to acknowledge the reality of your financial situation through honest self-assessment. Take stock of your bills, credit card statements, and loan agreements without judgment. Remember, awareness is crucial for change, much like the prodigal son in Luke 15:17 who recognized his situation and decided to return home.

Next, create a budget to serve as your financial roadmap towards becoming debt-free. Identify your income sources and categorize your expenses into essentials like housing and food, non-essentials like entertainment and dining out, and debt payments. Utilize budgeting tools such as apps and spreadsheets for added support on this journey.

Prioritizing debt repayment is essential. Treat your debt like a formidable opponent that requires taming. Begin by addressing high-interest debts first, employing methods like the snowball or avalanche technique. Every dollar saved for debt repayment brings you closer to financial freedom, much like gradually revealing a smooth surface beneath a large rock.

Resist the temptation of instant gratification. While impulsive purchases may provide fleeting pleasure, the resulting debt can linger. Remember the wisdom of delayed gratification, as Ecclesiastes 3:1 (ESV) suggests: "For everything there is a season, and a time for every matter under heaven."

Embrace frugality as a means to live within your means without sacrificing enjoyment. Seek ways to reduce expenses creatively, such as cooking at home, exploring free community entertainment options, and embracing do-it-yourself projects. Remember, true wealth is found in experiences and meaningful connections, not possessions, as Matthew 6:20 (NIV) wisely states: "For where your treasure is, there your heart will be also."

Living debt-free within your means is a journey that requires self-awareness, discipline, and faith. It involves making intentional choices that reflect your values and priorities, regardless of external pressures or societal norms. By embracing simplicity, contentment, and prudent stewardship, you can experience true freedom and abundance in your financial life. It's about creating a solid foundation for the future, similar to building your house on a rock as described in Matthew 7:24-27.

Chapter 4

Save Wisely: Prepare for the Future"

"Dishonest money dwindles away, but whoever gathers money little by little makes it grow."
— Proverbs 13:11 (NIV)

Have you ever dreamt of a future free from financial worries? A future where unexpected and expected expenses don't send chills down your spine, and opportunities beckon with open arms? Expenses are truly inevitable in our daily lives, from paying bills to purchasing necessities to gifting. The constant pull of expenses can make living seem like a daunting task. It may appear that the culture of consumerism and the various temptations to spend money make it challenging to prioritize saving for the future. Despite these numerous expenses we encounter, it is crucial to understand something which we will be looking into as we continue in this chapter. Therefore, be rest assured that you're not alone. We all yearn for a sense of security and freedom, and the key to unlocking that door lies in two simple words: save wisely.

As you navigate through the twists and turns of life, saving often feels like an afterthought, it might seem overwhelming, just like a distant goal overshadowed by pressing needs and tempting desires. We most times prioritize instant gratification, lured by the latest gadgets and fleeting trends. Yet, the Bible offers a profound perspective, reminding us that saving isn't just about financial stability; it's an act of faith, responsibility, and love.

Proverbs 21:5 whispers, "The plans of the diligent lead to profit as surely as haste leads to poverty." Just like building a sturdy house requires planning and forethought, building a secure future demands wise saving. It's not about deprivation, but about responsible choices that nurture a garden of financial security.

Recall the parable of the wise and foolish builders in Matthew 7:24-27? One built his house on a solid foundation, weathering the rain and floods, while the other's hastily built structure crumbled. This parable perfectly illustrates the importance of wise saving. By building a strong financial foundation through saving, we prepare ourselves for life's uncertainties, whether it's an unexpected car repair, a fire outbreak, a job loss, or even a dream vacation. As Proverbs 21:20 (CEV) reminds us, "Be sensible and store up precious treasures--don't waste them like a fool.."

Imagine tending a vibrant garden, nurturing seeds into blossoming abundance. That's the essence of saving wisely. Today's small contributions become tomorrow's bountiful harvest, empowering you to weather life's storms, pursue your dreams, and even bless others. The Bible implores us to be good stewards of our resources, to plan ahead for the future, and to be diligent in our financial affairs. Again in Proverbs 21:20 (NLT), "The wise have wealth and luxury, but fools spend whatever they get."

When we talk about saving wisely, it goes beyond simply setting aside money for a rainy day. It involves making intentional choices that align with your long-term goals and aspirations. Just as the ant prepares in the summer for the winter ahead (Proverbs 6:6-8), we too must be proactive in securing our financial well-being.

Imagine a carpenter diligently measuring and cutting wood to build a sturdy house. In the same way, you must carefully plan and allocate your resources to construct a strong financial foundation. Begin by calculating your total monthly income from all sources, including wages, salaries, and any additional sources of revenue then continue with another key aspect which is Budgeting.

Budgeting is a fundamental pillar for smart saving. It plays a crucial role in helping you manage your finances effectively. It acts as your financial guide, directing you towards your objectives and assisting you in making well-informed financial choices. By creating and sticking to a budget, you establish a plan for your money, ensuring that you allocate funds wisely and prioritize your financial goals.

When it comes to budgeting, one key aspect is tracking your expenses. Consider using a spreadsheet or a budgeting app to monitor where your money is going. Explore popular budgeting apps such as Mint, YNAB (You Need a Budget), or Personal Capital, which offer user-friendly interfaces and features for tracking expenses and managing cash flow. You can as well consider using Online Budgeting Templates such as Microsoft Excel templates, Google Sheets, or printable PDF templates.

This simple habit can provide valuable insights into your spending patterns and highlight areas where you may be overspending. Take a critical look at your recurring subscriptions. Do you think it is necessary for you to have multiple streaming services, gym memberships, or magazine subscriptions? Cancel unused ones, negotiate lower rates for others, or consider cheaper alternatives. Remember, every little bit saved adds up! For example, you might realize that you're spending more on dining out than you had anticipated or you are giving out even more than you are earning.

In your journey towards financial well-being, one of the most crucial steps we can take is to set clear and meaningful Financial Goals. Just as a ship needs a destination to sail towards, your financial plans require direction and purpose. Financial goals serve as your roadmap, guiding you towards the future you envision for yourself and your loved ones. They provide clarity, focus, and motivation to make wise financial decisions in the present. Without clear goals, one may drift aimlessly, susceptible to the whims of impulse. When setting financial goals, it's essential to think not only about what we want to achieve but also why it matters to us.

Ensure that your objectives are clear, quantifiable, attainable, pertinent, and tied to a deadline following the SMART criteria. (Specific, Measurable, Achievable, Relevant, and Time-bound). For example, rather than simply aiming to "save more money," a SMART goal might be to "save $10,000 for a down payment on a home within the next two years." Whether you aim to build an emergency fund, pay off debt, or save for a major purchase, having specific goals can help you stay motivated and focused. For instance, if your goal is to save for a vacation, you can create a separate savings category in your budget dedicated to this objective.

Personally, saving wisely means 'earning wisely'. It is a principle that emphasizes the importance of earning income strategically and efficiently in order to maximize your ability to save and achieve financial goals. There are several ways to earn extra income and bolster your savings such as embracing the Gig Economy, which provides flexible opportunities to showcase talents and skills on platforms like Upwork, Fiverr, or TaskRabbit. Alternatively, local gigs such as tutoring or pet-sitting can also bring in additional cash flow. Negotiate fair compensation for your work, salary or setting freelance rates.

To further increase income, a critical assessment of recurring expenses is essential. Trim down unnecessary subscriptions, negotiate for better rates, or seek cost-effective alternatives to optimize savings.

Automation stands out as a potent instrument in our pursuit of financial stability and prosperity as we plan to save wisely. It plays a critical role in our journey, offering significant advantages as we strive to achieve our goals. By automating your savings, you can make the process of setting aside money easier, more consistent, and less prone to procrastination or temptation. Automating savings is a manifestation of diligence in our financial stewardship. By setting up automatic transfers or contributions, you are proactively prioritizing your financial goals and ensuring that they are consistently funded, regardless of distractions or competing demands. The beauty of modern technology lies in its ability to make tasks easier.

You may want to identify the accounts where you'll be automating your savings. This may include a traditional savings account, a high-yield savings account, a retirement account like IRAs and 401(k)s or an investment account.

Then, you will need to calculate your savings rate. Determine the percentage of your income that you'd like to save each month. Financial experts often recommend saving at least 10% to 20% of your income, but the right savings rate will depend on your individual circumstances and goals.

Set up Automatic Transfers. Most banks and financial institutions offer the option to set up automatic transfers between accounts. Log in to your online banking platform or contact your bank to schedule recurring transfers from your checking account to your savings or investment accounts.

Strategically, you can utilize Employer-Sponsored Retirement Plans. If your employer offers a retirement savings plan such as a 401(k) or 403(b), take advantage of automatic contributions directly from your paycheck. These contributions are typically deducted pre-tax, reducing your taxable income and helping your savings grow faster.

For long-term savings goals, such as retirement, education expenses for you or your kids, consider setting up automatic investment plans (AIPs). AIPs allow you to automatically invest a fixed amount of money into mutual funds, exchange-traded funds (ETFs), or other investment vehicles on a regular basis. While automating savings provides convenience and consistency, it's essential to monitor your accounts regularly and adjust your savings strategy as needed. Review your financial goals periodically, reassess your savings rate, and make any necessary changes to ensure that you're on track to achieve your objectives. Remember, as the wise Benjamin Franklin observed, "A penny saved is a penny earned." Even small, regular contributions can yield surprising results over time.

For a more hands-on approach, challenge yourself with "**No-Spend**" days periodically. Dedicate specific days each week or month to avoid unnecessary spending. Explore free entertainment options like visiting museums on free days, picnicking in the park, or having game nights with friends. Challenge yourself to be creative and rediscover the joy of simple pleasures. By exploring cost-free leisure activities and curbing needless expenditures, you can discover simple joys without breaking the bank.

Adopting a minimalist mindset by selling unused items can also be lucrative. Organize garage sales, utilize online marketplaces, or explore consignment shops to convert clutter into cash, declutter your surroundings, and amass valuable savings.

Embarking on a "Savings Challenge" with friends or family could infuse fun into financial discipline. By choosing engaging themes and tracking progress collectively, this approach not only fosters motivation but can also turn savings into an enjoyable group activity.

Another approach is to set up an emergency fund to cover unexpected expenses like car repairs or medical bills. By having a financial safety net in place, you can avoid going into debt and protect yourself from financial setbacks.

Lastly on this chapter, Celebrate Your Wins! Every dollar saved is a victory, a step towards a secure future. Acknowledge your progress, reward yourself with experiences that enrich your life, and maintain a positive outlook on your journey. Remember, as Hebrews 6:10 (ESV) encourages, "For God is not unjust so as to overlook your work and the love you have shown for his name in serving the saints, as you still do." Celebrate your efforts, big and small, and stay motivated on your path to financial well-being.

Chapter 5
Invest Diligently: Multiply Your Resources"

"Give a portion to seven, or even to eight, for you know not what disaster may happen on earth."
– Ecclesiastes 11:2 (ESV)

Investing has always been a topic that stirs up various emotions and concerns among people. Investments essentially involve putting money or resources into assets with the expectation of generating profits or seeing an increase in value over time. This can be understood as using financial resources and assets in a thoughtful and strategic manner. It involves making decisions to allocate money into ventures or opportunities with the intention of earning a return or profit in the future.

People invest for various reasons – to grow their wealth, save for retirement, reach financial goals, or simply beat inflation. The world of investments offers a plethora of options, each with its unique risk-return profile.

Many people often confuse saving with investing, but there is a crucial difference between the two. Saving involves setting aside a portion of your income for future use without taking much risk, typically through a savings account or certificates of deposit. On the other hand, investing entails putting your money into vehicles like stocks, bonds, real estate, or mutual funds with the expectation of earning a return over time that outpaces inflation.

When we look at Proverbs 21:20 (ESV), it reminds us, "Precious treasure and oil are in a wise man's dwelling, but a foolish man devours it" teaching us the importance of not only saving but also wisely investing our resources. Just as the wise man preserves his treasure, so should we seek to grow our wealth through prudent investments.
Investing goes beyond the mere pursuit of financial gain; it is a pathway to financial freedom, security, and the ability to leave a lasting legacy for your loved ones. Imagine a future where you can retire comfortably, travel the world, or pursue your passions without financial constraints – that is the promise of diligent investing.

Consider the parable of the talents in Matthew 25:14-30, where a master entrusts his servants with different amounts of money to invest. The servants who wisely invested their talents were rewarded, while the one who buried his talent out of fear faced consequences. This story illustrates the importance of stewardship and making the most of the resources we are given.

One of the most compelling reasons to invest diligently is the prospect of achieving financial freedom. By building a diversified investment portfolio over time, you create a source of passive income that can sustain you beyond your working years. Whether it's through dividends, rental income, or capital gains, investing allows you to generate wealth that works for you while you sleep.

Think of the oak tree that grows strong and resilient over the years, providing shade and shelter to those around it. In the same way, your investments can grow steadily, offering you a secure foundation for a prosperous future.

By investing wisely, you are not only securing your own future but also that of your loved ones. Imagine being able to send your children to college without financial strain, care for aging parents, or leave an inheritance that will bless generations to come. The decisions you make now can influence the impact you leave for the future.

In 1 Timothy 5:8 (NIV) we are reminded, "Anyone who does not provide for their relatives, and especially for their own household, has denied the faith and is worse than an unbeliever." This verse underscores the importance of taking responsibility for the well-being of our families by making wise financial decisions like preparing for the future through investing.

Investment has long·been associated with a range of emotional responses and worries due to its inherent uncertainties. The fear of risk, lack of knowledge, and potential scams are valid concerns that often prevent individuals from taking the leap into the world of investing. These concerns are completely understandable given the complexities of the financial markets and the myriad of investment options available. However, it is essential to address these concerns head-on to make informed decisions and potentially reap the rewards that investing can offer.

One common fear that often holds people back from investing is the fear of risk. It's natural to feel apprehensive about putting your hard-earned money into investments that may fluctuate in value. However, it's crucial to understand that all investments carry some level of risk. The key is to manage that risk effectively by diversifying your investment portfolio and conducting thorough research before making any investment decisions. Remember, with risk comes the potential for reward, and taking calculated risks can lead to significant financial growth over time.

Many individuals also struggle with a lack of understanding when it comes to investing. Understanding complex financial concepts and navigating the intricacies of the stock market can be intimidating, especially for beginners. However, there are plenty of resources available to help educate yourself about investing, from online courses to books to financial advisors. By taking the time to increase your knowledge and understanding of investing, you can make more informed decisions and feel more confident in your investment strategy.

One of the biggest fears when it comes to investing is the potential for falling victim to scams, such as Ponzi schemes. Ponzi schemes are deceitful investment strategies that guarantee high profits while minimizing or claiming to eliminate risks. They operate by using new investors' money to pay returns to earlier investors, creating the illusion of profitability. However, Ponzi schemes are unsustainable and eventually collapse, leaving many investors with significant losses.

An infamous instance of a Ponzi scheme in the United States involves Bernie Madoff, who masterminded one of the most significant Ponzi schemes ever seen, swindling investors out of billions of dollars. The Madoff scandal underlines the vital importance of carrying out extensive due diligence and approaching investment prospects that appear overly promising with caution.

When it comes to navigating the world of investing, seeking wise counsel is crucial. Proverbs 15:22 reminds us that "Plans fail for lack of counsel, but with many advisers, they succeed." Consulting with financial professionals, such as financial advisors or investment experts, can provide valuable insights and help you make well-informed investment decisions. By seeking advice from those with experience and expertise in the field, you can better navigate the complexities of investing and mitigate potential risks.

Greed is another factor that can lead individuals astray when it comes to investing. The pursuit of quick profits and unsustainable returns can cloud judgment and lead to poor investment decisions. Proverbs 11:28 warns us that "Those who trust in their riches will fall, but the righteous will thrive like a green leaf." It's essential to approach investing with a mindset focused on long-term growth and financial stability rather than short-term gains driven by greed.

Investing can be a powerful tool for building wealth over time, but it can also be intimidating, especially for beginners. However, with the right approach, anyone can start investing with confidence. The key to successful investing lies in setting clear goals, conducting thorough research, choosing reputable brokers, starting small, diversifying your portfolio, and embracing sustainable investment practices.

Let's begin with setting investment goals. Before diving into the world of investing, take the time to define your financial objectives. Ask yourself questions such as: "What is my purpose of investment? Is it for retirement, buying a house, funding a child's education, or simply growing wealth?" Defining explicit investment objectives enables you to specify the duration of your investments and the extent of risk you are prepared to undertake.

Proverbs 13:11 (ESV) emphasizes the importance of diligent planning and setting financial goals: "Wealth gained hastily will dwindle, but whoever gathers little by little will increase it." This wise counsel underscores the value of patience and gradual accumulation when it comes to investing.

After setting your goals, the next step is to research different investment options. Educate yourself about various asset classes such as stocks, bonds, mutual funds, ETFs, real estate, and others which will still be explained in this book. Understand the risks associated with each investment type and how they align with your goals and risk tolerance.

Proverbs 24:3-4 (NIV) highlights the importance of acquiring knowledge before making investment decisions: "By wisdom a house is built, and through understanding, it is established; through knowledge, its rooms are filled with rare and beautiful treasures." Just like building a house requires careful planning and understanding, making informed investment choices can lead to valuable wealth accumulation.

When it comes to selecting a broker, opt for reputable and regulated financial institutions. Ensure the broker is licensed and has a good track record of customer service. Consider factors such as fees, account minimums, trading platforms, research tools, and customer support before making a decision.

Starting small is another crucial strategy for beginners. You don't need a significant amount of money to begin investing. Begin with an amount you are comfortable with and gradually increase your investments as you gain more confidence and see positive returns.

Diversification is a key principle in investing. Spread your investments among various types of assets to lower your risk exposure. Diversifying helps protect your portfolio from market fluctuations and minimizes potential losses in case a particular sector underperforms.

Proverbs 11:14 (NIV) emphasizes the wisdom of seeking advice from multiple sources: "For lack of guidance a nation falls, but victory is won through many advisers." In the context of investing, seeking diverse investment options and advice from financial experts can lead to a more robust and resilient portfolio.

Sustainable investing, also known as socially responsible investing, focuses on generating financial returns while contributing to social and environmental causes. Consider investing in companies that prioritize environmental sustainability, ethical practices, and social responsibility.
Additionally, be patient and maintain a long-term perspective in investing. The financial markets can be volatile, but historically, long-term investments have yielded positive returns. Avoid making impulsive decisions based on short-term market fluctuations and focus on your overarching financial goals.

Ecclesiastes 11:2 (NIV) encourages a forward-looking perspective in investments: "Invest in seven ventures, yes, in eight; you do not know what disaster may come upon the land." This verse underscores the importance of diversification and preparedness for unforeseen events in the investment journey.

Investing requires a blend of discipline, knowledge, patience, and a long-term mindset.

Now let's elucidate the range of investment options that exist, encompassing both traditional and contemporary choices.

Starting with one of the oldest and most traditional investment types – Real Estate. Investing in real estate involves purchasing properties such as houses, apartments, or commercial buildings with the aim of earning rental income or capital appreciation. Real estate is considered a tangible asset, meaning you own something physical. While real estate can provide stable returns through rental income and property value appreciation, it also comes with risks like market volatility, maintenance costs, and liquidity issues (as properties are not easily converted to cash).

Another classic investment avenue is stocks. When you buy shares of a company's stock, you essentially own a piece of that company. Stocks are considered one of the most dynamic investment options, offering the potential for high returns but also carrying significant risks. Stock prices can fluctuate widely based on company performance, economic conditions, and market sentiment. As a stock investor, you're exposed to market volatility, company-specific risk, and the risk of losing your entire investment if a company goes bankrupt.

Bonds are another traditional investment instrument. When you invest in bonds, you are essentially lending money to a corporation or government in exchange for periodic interest payments and the return of the principal amount at maturity. Bonds are typically seen as having lower risk compared to stocks, although they also come with reduced potential for earning high returns. The risk associated with bonds includes interest rate risk, credit risk (the risk of the issuer defaulting), and inflation risk (where inflation erodes the real value of your fixed income).

Moving into more contemporary investment options, we have exchange-traded funds (ETFs). ETFs are funds for investing that are traded on stock exchanges just like individual stocks. Usually, they follow an index, commodity, or a group of assets. ETFs offer diversification benefits, low costs, and ease of trading. However, they still carry market risks and are subject to price fluctuations based on their underlying assets.

Cryptocurrencies have gained significant popularity in recent years as a new form of investment. Bitcoin, Ethereum, Litecoin, XRP and other cryptocurrencies operate on blockchain technology and are known for their high volatility. While some investors have made substantial profits from crypto investments, the market is highly speculative and can be subject to regulatory changes, security risks, and technological challenges.

Peer-to-peer lending platforms have emerged as an alternative investment option, allowing individuals to lend money directly to borrowers through online platforms. These platforms offer the potential for higher returns compared to traditional fixed-income investments but also entail credit risk, liquidity risk, and platform-specific risks.

Lastly, we have alternative investments like hedge funds, private equity, and venture capital. These investments are typically reserved for accredited investors and institutions due to their complex nature and higher risk profile. Alternative investments can provide diversification benefits and potentially higher returns but often come with limited liquidity, high minimum investment requirements, and less regulatory oversight.

The world of investments is vast and diverse, offering various options to suit different risk appetites and financial goals. Whether you choose traditional assets like real estate and stocks or explore newer avenues like cryptocurrencies and peer-to-peer lending, it's crucial to conduct thorough research, understand the associated risks, and consider seeking advice from financial professionals. Remember, there's no one-size-fits-all approach to investing, and diversification is key to building a strong investment portfolio.

While investing, uncertainties and risks are unavoidable. This is where trust in God comes into play. Proverbs 3:5-6 (NIV) instructs us to "Trust in the Lord with all your heart and lean not on your own understanding; in all your ways submit to him, and he will make your paths straight." This verse underscores the significance of having faith in God's direction over depending solely on our own understanding or research. When we trust in God, we acknowledge that there are greater forces at work in our lives, especially when it comes to handling our finances and investments.

When investing, it's crucial to align our values and beliefs with our financial decisions. We, as Christians, are summoned to responsibly manage the resources that have been given to us. Proverbs 21:20 (NIV) states, "The wise store up choice food and olive oil, but fools gulp theirs down." This verse highlights the importance of prudent planning and wise investments. By aligning our investments with our values—such as supporting ethical companies, businesses that promote social responsibility, or those that align with our moral convictions—we not only earn returns but also contribute to making a positive impact in the world.

Moreover, using our resources for good reflects our commitment to being agents of positive change. 1 Timothy 6:17-19 (NIV) "Command those who are rich in this present world not to be arrogant nor to put their hope in wealth, which is so uncertain, but to put their hope in God, who richly provides us with everything for our enjoyment. Command them to do good, to be rich in good deeds, and to be generous and willing to share. In this way, they will lay up treasure for themselves as a firm foundation for the coming age so that they may take hold of the life that is truly life." This excerpt highlights the significance of utilizing our financial assets to help others and create a lasting influence that extends beyond our individual lifetime.

When we integrate faith into our investment journey, we are not just pursuing financial success; we are also seeking to honor God with our resources and make a positive difference in the world. By trusting in God's guidance, aligning our investments with our values, and using our resources for good, we can cultivate a sense of purpose and fulfillment in our financial endeavors.

Taking this approach requires a mindset shift—from viewing investments as solely a means to accumulate wealth to seeing them as opportunities to make a meaningful impact. It's a transformation that goes beyond mere financial gains; it encompasses a holistic view of wealth that includes spiritual, ethical, and social considerations.

So, stay informed, stay curious, and embark on your investment journey with a blend of prudence and optimism. Remember to seek guidance from God, exercise discernment in your financial decisions, and align your actions with principles of integrity and wisdom found in the Word. Ultimately, strive to use your resources in ways that honor God and benefit others.

Chapter 6

Seek Counsel: Make Informed Financial Decisions

"Plans fail for lack of counsel, but with many advisers, they succeed."
– Proverbs 15:22 (NIV)

Consider that you might be going through a major life transition such as marriage, parenthood, or retirement, which can significantly impact your financial situation. You might be grappling with questions like, "How can we merge our finances as a couple?" or "Am I financially prepared for retirement?" or "How do we keep up with housing expenses and School bills for the kids?"

Let's say you are a small business owner looking to expand your operations but unsure about the financial risks involved. Questions may arise in your mind like, "How can I secure funding for growth without compromising the stability of my business?" You might be wondering, "How can I best manage my finances to secure a stable business future?" In moments like these, seeking guidance from a financial advisor can provide valuable insights and strategies to set you on the right path.

In the book of Proverbs 15:22 (NIV), it says, "Plans fail for lack of counsel, but with many advisers, they succeed." This is where financial counsel can play a crucial role in helping you assess the risks, explore financing options, and develop a solid financial plan for growth.

Reflecting on 1 Corinthians 16:2 (ESV): "On the first day of every week, each of you is to put something aside and store it up, as he may prosper, so that there will be no collecting when I come." We are reminded of the importance of prudent financial management. Seeking guidance to allocate resources wisely and plan for the future aligns with this biblical principle of stewardship.

At this point, seeking guidance from a financial advisor can help you navigate these transitions smoothly and make informed decisions that align with your goals.

Making informed financial decisions is crucial for achieving financial stability and growth. Seeking counsel in managing your finances wisely can be a game-changer. It involves seeking advice from financial experts or trusted individuals who can provide guidance tailored to your specific needs and goals. By seeking counsel, you gain valuable insights and perspectives that can help you make informed choices about saving, investing, and budgeting. Remember, seeking counsel is not a sign of weakness but a wise decision-making strategy. It shows that you value your financial well-being and are willing to learn and improve.

Navigating personal finances can often feel overwhelming and intimidating, requiring a blend of practical knowledge and the timeless wisdom found in scripture. In seeking counsel for making informed financial decisions, there is a treasure trove of guidance waiting to be discovered.

Think about Proverbs 15:22 from the New International Version, "Plans fail for lack of counsel, but with many advisers, they succeed." This verse underscores the importance of seeking counsel when making decisions, especially those concerning finances. Just as in the Bible, it's essential for us to seek wise counsel from trusted sources when navigating our financial journeys.

So, what does it actually mean to seek counsel? Seeking counsel involves humbly acknowledging that we don't have all the answers and being open to perspectives that can help us make better decisions. It means approaching those with more experience or expertise in financial matters and learning from them. Seeking counsel is not a sign of weakness but a display of wisdom and humility.

As you journey through the realm of personal finances, it's crucial to make informed decisions. Ephesians 5:15-16 ESV again advises, "Look carefully then how you walk, not as unwise but as wise, making the best use of the time, because the days are evil." This verse implores us to be wise and deliberate in our decision-making, especially in financial matters which can significantly impact our lives.

Making informed financial decisions involves thorough research, understanding risks and rewards, setting clear goals, and seeking advice when needed. It means being disciplined in budgeting, saving, investing wisely, and avoiding impulsive spending. By staying informed and educated about financial matters, you empower yourself to make choices that align with your goals and values.

Furthermore, Proverbs 13:11 in the New American Standard Bible warns, "Wealth obtained by fraud dwindles, but the one who gathers by labor increases it." This verse reminds us of the importance of ethical behavior in our pursuit of financial stability. Making informed financial decisions also entails acting with integrity, honesty, and diligence in all our financial dealings.

As you connect the dots between seeking counsel and making informed financial decisions, remember that knowledge without guidance can lead to missteps, just as seeking counsel without practical action can result in stagnation. By integrating both aspects, you pave the way for a balanced and fruitful financial journey guided by wisdom and prudence.

Seeking guidance from qualified financial advisors for complex situations or specialized needs is a wise decision that can have a significant impact on your financial well-being. Just like seeking advice from experts in other areas of your life, consulting with professionals in the field of finance can provide you with valuable insights, strategies, and solutions tailored to your specific circumstances.

Think of financial advisors as your trusted partners on the journey towards financial prosperity and security. They bring a wealth of knowledge, experience, and expertise to the table, helping you navigate through the complexities of investments, taxes, retirement planning, estate planning, and more. By tapping into their specialized skills, you can make informed decisions that align with your financial goals and aspirations.

In the book of Proverbs 15:22 (NIV), it is written, "Plans fail for lack of counsel, but with many advisers, they succeed." This verse highlights the importance of seeking counsel and guidance from multiple sources when making important decisions. Just as seeking advice from wise counselors can lead to success in various aspects of life, seeking guidance from qualified financial advisors can lead to success in managing your finances effectively.

Qualified financial advisors can help you develop a comprehensive financial plan that addresses your short-term and long-term goals, identifies potential risks, and maximizes opportunities for growth. They can assist you in creating a balanced investment portfolio, managing your cash flow, optimizing your tax strategy, and preparing for significant life milestones like purchasing a house, launching a business, or setting money aside for your kids' education.

In the book of Proverbs 24:6 (NIV), it is written, "Surely you need guidance to wage war, and victory is won through many advisers." This verse emphasizes the power of seeking guidance and counsel from knowledgeable individuals when facing challenges or pursuing goals. In the realm of personal finance, the "war" is the journey towards financial stability and prosperity, and the "advisers" are the qualified professionals who can equip you with the tools and strategies needed to achieve victory.

When it comes to complex financial situations or specialized needs, seeking advice from qualified financial advisors is not a sign of weakness, but a sign of wisdom and strength. These professionals have the expertise and resources to help you overcome obstacles, capitalize on opportunities, and make informed decisions that can have a positive impact on your financial future.

It is important to remember that financial planning is not a one-size-fits-all process. What works for one person may not work for another, which is why personalized guidance from a qualified financial advisor is essential. By sharing your unique goals, concerns, and circumstances with a professional advisor, you can receive personalized recommendations and tailored solutions that meet your individual needs.

According to Proverbs 11:14 (NIV), it is written, "For lack of guidance a nation falls, but victory is won through many advisers." This line emphasizes the importance of looking for guidance and counsel from a diverse group of advisers to achieve success and avoid pitfalls. In the context of personal finance, seeking guidance from qualified financial advisors can help you avoid costly mistakes, mitigate risks, and stay on course towards financial success.

There are various types of financial advisors out there, each catering to different needs and goals, so finding the right one for you is crucial. It's like choosing the perfect partner who understands your dreams and aspirations, guiding you towards a brighter financial future.

Let's dive into the fascinating realm of financial advisors and uncover how you can identify the one that suits you best.

First, we have the ever-wise and experienced Certified Financial Planners (CFPs). These folks are like seasoned mentors in the financial advisory world, equipped with comprehensive knowledge and skills to tackle a variety of financial situations. If you're looking for holistic advice on investments, retirement planning, tax strategies, and more, a CFP might be your best bet.

Next up are the Registered Investment Advisors (RIAs), known for their fiduciary duty to act in your best interest. They don't just throw around generic advice; they tailor their recommendations specifically to your needs. Think of them as your personal financial architects, designing a sturdy financial blueprint to secure your future.

Then there's the charming group known as the Robo-Advisors, the tech-savvy solution for those who prefer a hands-off approach. These digital platforms use algorithms to optimize your investments based on your risk tolerance and financial objectives. It's like having a digital buddy who keeps a watchful eye on your finances 24/7.

Lastly, we can't forget about the good ol' Investment Brokers. While some may possess flashy sales skills, it's essential to discern between those who truly have your best interests at heart versus those simply chasing hefty commissions. Remember, not all that glitters is gold, so choose wisely.

How do you identify a qualified financial advisor amidst these diverse sea of options?
First and foremost, look for certifications like CFP, ChFC (Chartered Financial Consultant), or CFA (Chartered Financial Analyst). These titles signal that your advisor has put in the time and effort to specialize in financial planning and investment management.

Additionally, consider their track record and experience in handling situations similar to yours. A solid history of helping clients achieve their financial goals is a good indicator of their expertise. Don't hesitate to ask for references or testimonials to verify their credibility.

When you sit down for that initial consultation, pay close attention to how well they listen to your goals and concerns. A great advisor should be a great listener first and foremost, understanding your unique circumstances before tailoring a plan that fits like a glove.

Lastly, trust your gut instinct. If something seems suspicious or too perfect to be true, chances are it is. Your financial advisor should be someone you feel comfortable with, someone you can trust to guide you through the complexities of investment decisions and financial planning.

When working with a competent financial advisor, Clear communication and transparency are absolutely crucial. It's vital to ensure that you understand each other and are on the same page every step of the way. Being open, honest, and asking questions can make all the difference in achieving your financial goals."

Investing time and effort into establishing clear communication with your financial advisor can lead to a more productive and successful partnership. Make sure you express your financial goals, concerns, and expectations openly. Remember, transparency is key in building trust and ensuring that you are making informed decisions about your financial future. Regularly review your financial plan and performance to stay informed and engaged in the process. Ultimately, effective communication can empower you to make sound financial choices and secure a more stable financial future."

Choosing the right financial advisor is akin to finding a companion on your journey to financial success. It's about building a relationship based on trust, expertise, and mutual understanding of your goals. Take your time, do your research, and don't settle for anything less than the perfect match for your financial needs. Your future self will give you a thumbs up for this.

Chapter 7

Work Diligently: Value Labor and Earn Income"

"Lazy people are soon poor; hard workers get rich"
– Proverbs 10:4 (NLT)

In life, there is profound wisdom in appreciating the value of work, embracing a diligent mindset, and understanding how labor contributes to both personal fulfillment and financial security. The Bible emphasizes the importance of work ethic and diligence in several passages. In Colossians 3:23-24 (NIV), it is written: "Whatever you do, work at it with all your heart, as working for the Lord, not for human masters, since you know that you will receive an inheritance from the Lord as a reward. It is the Lord Christ you are serving."

By internalizing this message, we can see work as a means of expressing our faith and dedication, regardless of the task at hand. This outlook transforms mundane jobs into opportunities to showcase our commitment and integrity. Moreover, the pursuit of excellence in our work not only brings a sense of personal satisfaction but also paves the way for long-term success and financial stability.

Proverbs 12:24 (ESV) affirms this by stating: "The hand of the diligent will rule, while the slothful will be put to forced labor." This passage underscores the correlation between industriousness and achieving personal goals. When we apply ourselves diligently to our work, we position ourselves for leadership roles and greater influence in our spheres of influence. Diligence is not merely about working hard but also about working smart and with purpose.

Furthermore, Ecclesiastes 9:10 (NLT) reminds us: "Whatever you do, do well. For when you go to the grave, there will be no work or planning or knowledge or wisdom." This verse acts as a strong encouragement for us to exert our utmost effort in all our pursuits, understanding that our present actions influence our lasting legacy and affect the generations to come.

In essence, our approach to work reflects our values, character, and ambitions. When we embrace a diligent mindset and strive for excellence in our labor, we align ourselves with the divine purpose of contributing positively to the world around us. Work becomes more than just a means to an end; it becomes a channel through which we can express our creativity, serve others, and fulfill our unique calling.

As we navigate the intricacies of work and labor, let us remember the words of 1 Corinthians 15:58 (NLT): "So, my dear brothers and sisters, be strong and immovable. Always work enthusiastically for the Lord, for you know that nothing you do for the Lord is ever useless." This passage encourages us to strive with excellence in everything we do, understanding that our present actions mold our heritage and influence the future, knowing that our efforts are never in vain when done with a pure heart and a steadfast spirit.

Diligence in work is like adding extra sprinkles on your favorite dessert—it elevates the whole experience and makes it truly special. It's a mix of dedication, perseverance, and integrity, all rolled into one shiny ball of excellence. Picture yourself in the shoes of a gifted craftsman, pouring your heart and soul into every stroke of the brush or every line of code you write. That's diligence—it's not just about getting the job done, but about doing it with a spirit of excellence that sets you apart. The journey of appreciating the value of work, embracing diligence, and understanding the link between labor and personal fulfillment is an ongoing process.

Throughout history, work has played a vital role in human flourishing and contributing to society. Imagine a world where no one worked—no progress, no innovation, no growth. It would be uninteresting and quite dull, don't you think?

Now, let's talk about the importance of work in our lives. Think about it this way: work is not just about earning a paycheck. It's about finding purpose, honing skills, and making a difference. When you engage in meaningful work, you not only improve your own life but also contribute positively to society. Your work can be like a ripple effect, creating impact far beyond what you may realize.

Consider the historical perspective on work and labor. Back in the day, people worked primarily for survival. They tilled the land, crafted tools, and built shelters to meet their basic needs. As societies evolved, work took on new dimensions—artisans creating beautiful crafts, scholars sharing knowledge, and inventors revolutionizing industries. Each person's labor added to the collective progress of humanity.

Fast forward to today, and we find ourselves in a world driven by technology and innovation. Working has become more diverse and interconnected than ever before. Whether you're a teacher shaping young minds, a doctor saving lives, or an entrepreneur bringing new ideas to life, your work matters. It's a part of the intricate web that sustains and enriches our society thereby making you earn an income. Money makes the world go 'round, as they say. Earning income is essential for meeting your needs, supporting your families, and pursuing your dreams but it's not just about the numbers in your bank account. It's about the value you bring to the table, the impact you create, and the life you build for yourself.

Looking back at the dawn of creation in Genesis 2:15, we see God placing Adam in the lush garden of Eden "...to work it and take care of it." Here, work wasn't a punishment or a necessary evil—it was part of God's original design for humanity. Think about it: tending to the garden wasn't just about pulling weeds and watering plants; it was about stewarding God's creation with love and care, bringing order out of chaos, and cultivating beauty in the world.

When you view work through this biblical lens, you start to see it as a powerful tool for shaping not just your own life but also the world around you. Your diligence in work becomes a force for good, contributing to the flourishing of society and the advancement of God's kingdom here on earth. Whether you're a teacher shaping young minds, a doctor healing the sick, or an artist creating beauty, your work has the potential to inspire, uplift, and transform lives.

God doesn't want you to underestimate the power of your diligence in work. He wants you to embrace it as a sacred calling, a way to honor Him and serve others with excellence. Let your dedication, perseverance, and integrity shine brightly in everything you do, knowing that you are contributing to something much bigger than yourself.

Struggling with diligence at work is a common challenge that many people face. The feeling of boredom can creep in when tasks become too routine or unexciting. It's easy to feel drained and fatigued, especially when faced with long hours or repetitive work. Feeling undervalued at work can also contribute to a lack of motivation and effort.

But here's the thing, we are meant to overcome challenges! When you find yourself procrastinating or getting distracted, remember the rewards that come with focused effort and dedication. Each task you complete, each project you excel in, brings you one step closer to achieving your goals and earning the income you deserve. Your labor is valuable, and your hard work will not go unnoticed.

In the Bible, Proverbs 14:23 (NIV) reminds us, "All hard work brings a profit, but mere talk leads only to poverty." This verse serves as a powerful motivation to push through challenges and strive for excellence in all that we do. Your commitment to diligent work will lead you to success and abundance, both in your career and personal fulfillment.

When boredom starts to set in, try to find ways to make your tasks more engaging. Challenge yourself to approach familiar tasks from a new perspective or set small goals to keep yourself motivated. Break down large projects into smaller, manageable tasks to avoid feeling overwhelmed and maintain a sense of progress.

Combatting fatigue requires taking care of yourself both physically and mentally. Ensure you're getting enough rest, staying hydrated, and taking breaks when needed. Implementing short exercise routines or mindfulness practices can help boost your energy levels and focus.

Feeling undervalued can be disheartening, but remember that your work has worth and significance. Communicate with your supervisors about your contributions and accomplishments, and don't hesitate to ask for feedback or recognition when it's due. Seek out opportunities for growth and skill development to further showcase your value to the organization.

As you navigate through these challenges, keep your eyes on the prize – the satisfaction of knowing that your hard work will yield rewards, both personally and professionally. Stay dedicated to your goals, remain focused on the task at hand, and embrace the journey towards success with tenacity and resilience.

Remember that every effort you put in today is an investment in a brighter tomorrow. Your diligence will pave the way for greater opportunities and fulfillment. You need to rise above procrastination and distractions, embrace the joy of focused effort, and let your dedication shine through in all that you do. Your labor is valuable, and your commitment will lead you to the rewards you deserve especially when your work aligns your passion.

Discovering work that aligns with your personal values and passions is like striking gold in the realm of career fulfillment. It's the secret ingredient to finding meaning, purpose, and yes, even financial success. Picture yourself waking up every morning excited to start your day because you know that the work you do truly matters to you and others. Imagine feeling a deep sense of satisfaction because you're not just going through the motions, but actually living out your purpose. That's the power of aligning your work with what you value and love.

Think about it when you do something you're truly passionate about, you naturally put in your best effort. Your enthusiasm shines through, and people notice. This, in turn, can lead to greater recognition, opportunities for growth, and ultimately, financial rewards. It's a win-win situation – you get to do what you love while also being rewarded for it. Who wouldn't want that?

"How can I determine my genuine passion?" You may wonder, the answer lies in exploring your unique combination of talents, skills, and interests. Take some time to reflect on what activities make you lose track of time, what topics you could talk about for hours on end, or what causes ignite a fire within you. These are clues pointing you towards work that resonates with your soul.

If you're unsure where to start, here are some current job trends that could align with different passions and values:

Digital Marketing Specialist: If you have a knack for creativity and a love for storytelling, a career in digital marketing could be your calling. You'll get to combine your passion for connecting with people with the ever-evolving digital landscape.

Life Coach or Mentor: Are you the friend that everyone turns to for advice and support? Consider becoming a life coach or mentor. You can help others unlock their potential and lead more fulfilling lives.

Sustainability Consultant: For those passionate about protecting the environment, a career as a sustainability consultant allows you to create positive change in the world while also making a living.

Nonprofit Manager: If making a difference in your community is high on your list of values, working for a nonprofit organization could be the perfect fit. You'll be contributing to a cause you believe in while also honing your leadership skills.

Nutritionist or Health Coach: If health and wellness are your passions, consider becoming a nutritionist or health coach. You'll have the opportunity to empower others to lead healthier lives while doing what you love.

Remember, it's never too late to pursue work that aligns with your values and passions. Your unique combination of talents and interests is what sets you apart and makes your contribution to the world special.

In the Bible, Colossians 3:23-24 (NIV) reminds us, "Whatever you do, work at it with all your heart, as working for the Lord, not for human masters, since you know that you will receive an inheritance from the Lord as a reward. It is the Lord Christ you are serving." This verse underscores the idea that our work, when done wholeheartedly and in alignment with our values, is not in vain. There is a greater purpose beyond just financial gain; our work can be a form of worship and service to God.

So, if you're feeling stuck in a job that doesn't resonate with who you are or what you believe in, take heart. You have the power to shape your career to reflect your values and passions. Trust in your unique abilities, explore new possibilities, and remember that your work has meaning and value, both in the eyes of God and for your own personal and financial fulfillment.

Embrace the journey of discovering work that brings you joy and fulfillment. Your passion, when paired with purpose, has the potential to create a ripple effect of positivity in both your life and the lives of those around you. Believe in yourself, trust in your journey, and let your light shine through the work you choose to do.

Chapter 8

"Practice Contentment: Be Grateful for What You Have"

"Keep your lives free from the love of money and be content with what you have, because God has said, 'Never will I leave you; never will I forsake you."
– Hebrews 13:5 (NIV)

There was a time when greed clouded my judgment, and I felt that I never had enough. Focused on saving more, I just wanted to digest everything in, and wanted to secure my future. I often lost sight of all the blessings surrounding me. It wasn't until God intervened, redirecting my steps and thoughts, that I finally realized the true importance of contentment and gratitude.

In a moment of clarity, I heard a gentle voice whisper, "My child, remember that wealth is not only measured in material possessions, but in the richness of your heart and soul. Be thankful for what you have and trust in my plan for you."

From that day on, I made a conscious effort to give thanks for both the good and the bad, knowing that every experience was a stepping stone towards growth and understanding. My heart overflowed with gratitude, and I found peace in the simple joys of life. In the hustle and bustle of daily life, in a world that constantly urges us to chase after more—more money, more success, more possessions, more power— it's easy to get swept up in the tide of discontentment and ingratitude. However, the key lies in recognizing the blessings around us and fostering a heart of thankfulness towards our Creator.

The Scriptures offer us a guiding light in this pursuit. In 1 Thessalonians 5:18 (NIV), we are urged to "give thanks in all circumstances; for this is God's will for you in Christ Jesus." These words remind us that gratitude is not merely a suggestion but a powerful act of obedience and faith. When we choose to give thanks in every situation, we align our hearts with God's will and open ourselves up to experience His provisions, peace and joy.

Contentment represents a deep sense of peace and fulfillment that comes from within, transcending mere satisfaction or fleeting happiness. It is an inner state of being where one accepts and appreciates their current circumstances, regardless of external factors. The book of Philippians 4:11-12 (NIV) echoes this sentiment, where the apostle Paul writes, "I have learned to be content whatever the circumstances. I know what it is to be in need, and I know what it is to have plenty. I have learned the secret of being content in any and every situation."

This verse illustrates the profound nature of contentment, showing that it is a learned behavior that can be cultivated through experiences and reflections. It conveys the idea that contentment is not dependent on external conditions but stems from an inner strength and perspective. Just as Paul found contentment in various situations, you too can learn to find peace and acceptance in your life.

Contentment empowers us to face life's hurdles with grace and resilience, fostering a sense of gratitude and tranquility that uplifts our spirits. It is a powerful state that allows us to appreciate the present moment and find joy in the simplest of things. Practicing contentment involves embracing a mindset of gratitude, letting go of unnecessary desires, and finding peace in the midst of life's uncertainties. In essence, contentment is a journey towards inner harmony and fulfillment that enriches our lives and nourishes our souls.

Gratitude is the foundation upon which contentment is built. When we practice gratitude, we train our minds to focus on the positives in our lives rather than dwelling on what we lack. It shifts our perspective from scarcity to abundance, helping us appreciate the simple joys and blessings that surround us each day. Fostering the act of gratitude is not just a one-time decision but a daily practice. In Philippians 4:6-7 (NIV), we are encouraged, "Do not be anxious about anything, but in every situation, by prayer and petition, with thanksgiving, present your requests to God. And the peace of God, which transcends all understanding, will guard your hearts and your minds in Christ Jesus." The interplay between gratitude, prayer, and the sense of tranquility provided by God in the face of life's trials is profoundly emphasized.

Moreover, Psalm 107:1 (NIV) reminds us to "give thanks to the Lord, for he is good; his love endures forever." We see a powerful proclamation of God's unchanging goodness and everlasting love towards us in this verse. When we meditate on God's goodness and faithfulness, our hearts naturally overflow with gratitude and praise, leading us to a deeper sense of contentment and joy.

It is essential to shift our focus from what we lack to the abundance of blessings that surround us. As stated in James 1:17 (NIV), "Every good and perfect gift is from above, coming down from the Father of the heavenly lights, who does not change like shifting shadows." God's steadfast and unchanging love for us is evident in the blessings He bestows upon us, including His guidance in managing our finances. This verse emphasizes that every good thing we experience is a gracious gift from God, reflecting His constant care and provision in every aspect of our lives.

Furthermore, Colossians 3:15 (NIV) encourages us to "let the peace of Christ rule in your hearts, since as members of one body you were called to peace. And be thankful" emphasizing the role of gratitude in inviting the peace of Christ to reign in our hearts. When we approach life with a spirit of thankfulness, we create space for God's peace to guard our emotions and thoughts, leading to a profound sense of contentment and fulfillment.

Contentment vs Complacency

Contentment and complacency may seem similar at first glance, but they have stark differences that can impact our mindset, actions, and overall well-being. Let's dive deeper into these concepts by exploring how they relate to gratitude and appreciation.

Contentment reflects a state of satisfaction and peace within oneself regardless of external circumstances. It involves embracing what we have without longing for more. In essence, contentment is about finding joy and fulfillment in the present moment, appreciating the blessings and gifts that surround us. The Bible encourages us to cultivate contentment in various verses. For instance, in Philippians 4:11-12 (NIV), the apostle Paul writes, "I have learned to be content whatever the circumstances. I know what it is to be in need, and I know what it is to have plenty. I have learned the secret of being content in any and every situation." This verse highlights the significance of maintaining contentment regardless of the ups and downs in life.

On the other hand, complacency entails a sense of self-satisfaction that hinders growth and improvement. It involves settling for mediocrity and being stagnant in one's journey. Complacent individuals may resist change, neglect personal development, and be unmotivated to strive for betterment. The Bible warns against complacency in Revelations 3:15-16 (NLT), where it states, "I know all the things you do, that you are neither hot nor cold. I wish that you were one or the other! But since you are like lukewarm water, neither hot nor cold, I will spit you out of my mouth!" This passage underscores the dangers of being lukewarm and complacent in one's faith and actions.

Gratitude and appreciation serve as key components in distinguishing between contentment and complacency. Practicing gratitude involves recognizing and acknowledging the good in our lives, fostering a positive outlook and sense of abundance. When we express gratitude, we shift our focus from what is lacking to what we have been blessed with, fostering a sense of contentment. As the Psalmist proclaims in Psalm 106:1 (NIV), "Praise the Lord. Give thanks to the Lord, for he is good; his love endures forever." This verse highlights the transformative power of gratitude in acknowledging God's goodness and nurturing contentment.

Appreciation, on the other hand, involves valuing and recognizing the efforts of others, as well as the beauty and wonders around us. When we appreciate the people, experiences, and blessings in our lives, we cultivate a spirit of contentment that transcends mere satisfaction. The book of James underscores the importance of appreciation in James 1:17 (NLT), stating, "Whatever is good and perfect is a gift coming down to us from God our Father, who created all the lights in the heavens."

Importantly, you have got to shift your perspective of contentment into the power of reframing negative thoughts into the positive aspects of life. It's like what the Bible says in Philippians 4:8 (NIV), "Finally, brothers and sisters, whatever is true, whatever is noble, whatever is right, whatever is pure, whatever is lovely, whatever is admirable—if anything is excellent or praiseworthy—think about such things." This verse serves as a guide for us to steer our minds towards positivity, beauty, and goodness in the midst of life's challenges.

When negative thoughts start creeping in, it's crucial to pause and reflect. Ask yourself, "Is this thought true or just a product of my worries?" Reframing means looking at the situation from a different angle. Instead of focusing on what's seeming wrong, focus on what's looking right. Maybe you had a tough day at work, but you can be grateful for supportive colleagues or the skills you've developed. By shifting your perspective, you can find a silver lining even in the darkest clouds.

It's about training your mind to see the good In every situation. Even in moments of despair, there's always a glimmer of hope waiting to be noticed. Challenge yourself to find that spark of positivity, no matter how small. Remember, positivity attracts positivity. When you radiate good vibes, you invite more blessings into your life.

Choosing positivity doesn't mean ignoring reality. It means acknowledging the hardships but refusing to let them define you. Embrace a mindset of gratitude and resilience. Count your blessings, no matter how few they may seem. Every obstacle presents a chance for personal development and acquiring knowledge. Trust in the process, knowing that better days are ahead.

Practicing gratitude daily is like putting on a pair of glasses that help you see the world in a brighter light. Here are some effective strategy for practicing gratitude:

Journaling: Take a few minutes each day to write down things you are thankful for. It can be as simple as having a roof over your head, a warm cup of coffee in the morning, a kind word from a friend, to all profit realized or income and revenue generated over time. Penning down these blessings can shift your focus from what's lacking to what you already have.

Mindfulness exercises: These involve being fully present and aware of your thoughts, feelings, and surroundings without judgment. These exercises help you stay present in the moment and fully appreciate the blessings around you. Next time you sit down to eat a meal, pause for a moment to savor each bite. Notice the flavors, textures, and the effort that went into preparing the food. Mindful eating can help you feel grateful for the nourishment and enjoyment each meal brings. When it comes to money management, practicing mindfulness can help you make wiser financial decisions by being conscious of your spending habits, saving goals, and overall financial well-being without attaching negative emotions, such as anxiety or fear. This can create a sense of abundance and appreciation for the resources you have, leading to more responsible financial decisions and a healthier relationship with money.

Acknowledging small blessings throughout the day can also amplify your sense of gratitude. Whether it's a beautiful sunrise, a stranger's smile, a moment of peace and quiet, a successful profitable deal you closed or a raise in your wage, take the time to notice and appreciate these small moments. By cultivating awareness of these everyday gifts, you'll find yourself feeling more grateful for the beauty and goodness that surrounds you.

Psalms 106:1 (NIV), says, "Praise the Lord. Give thanks to the Lord, for he is good; his love endures forever." This verse reminds us that gratitude is a way to acknowledge and honor the goodness of life and the love that surrounds us. When we practice gratitude, we are not only expressing appreciation for what we have but also recognizing the source of all blessings.

As you journey through each day, remember to journal your blessings, practice mindfulness, and pay attention to the small joys around you. By incorporating these practices into your daily routine, you'll cultivate a heart full of gratitude and a spirit that overflows with thankfulness. Take a moment to reflect on the abundance in your life, and let gratitude be your guide to finding joy, fruitfulness and productivity in the ordinary moments.

Chapter 9

Be Patient: Trust in God's Timing for Financial Blessings"

"God's blessing makes life rich; nothing we do can improve on God."
– Proverbs 10:22 (MSG)

In our fast-paced world, it's easy to fall into the trap of wanting instant results, especially when it comes to our finances. We often desire control over our money, seeking to plan every detail meticulously. However, there is beauty in surrendering that control and placing our trust in a higher power—the divine and sovereign plan of God.

Proverbs 16:9 (NIV) says, "In their hearts humans plan their course, but the Lord establishes their steps." This verse beautifully encapsulates the timeless struggle between human desire for control and the divine orchestration of God's plan. We may carefully and strategically plan our financial goals, create budgets, and strive for success, but ultimately, it is God who paves the way and determines our ultimate path to financial blessings.

Think about it for a moment. How many times have you diligently planned your financial journey, only to face unexpected twists and turns along the way? It is during these times that our faith undergoes a true test. We are called to embrace patience and trust in God's divine timing, knowing that He has a perfect plan for each one of us.

You see, God operates on a different timetable than we do. While we may want immediate results and quick fixes to our financial challenges, God's timing is infinite and perfect. He sees the bigger picture, knows what lies ahead, and works all things together for our good. So, when it comes to financial blessings, it's essential to surrender our timelines and trust that God's plan is far greater than anything we could imagine.

Perhaps you are in a season of financial hardship or uncertainty right now. You might be questioning why things aren't progressing as quickly as you'd like. In those moments, I urge you to lean on your faith and trust in God's timing. Remember that waiting on God doesn't mean doing nothing—it means actively placing your trust in Him and aligning your actions with His will.

God's plan is dynamic and ever-unfolding. Just as a farmer must patiently wait for the seeds to grow into a bountiful harvest, we too must cultivate patience and trust in God's provision. Sometimes, the waiting period is where we experience the most growth and transformation, preparing us for the blessings that are yet to come.

Let go of the need for immediate results and embrace the journey of trusting in God's timing. It's not about controlling every aspect of your financial life; it's about surrendering to the divine plan that is already in motion. Be patient, have faith, and watch as God's blessings unfold in ways beyond your wildest dreams.

Patience is more than just waiting; it's a spiritual virtue that transcends mere endurance. It involves trusting in a higher power and accepting that things will happen in their own time, according to a divine plan. In the book of James in the Bible, it is written that we should rejoice when we encounter various trials because our faith being tested leads to developing perseverance and we should let perseverance finish its work so that we may be mature and complete, not lacking anything." This passage emphasizes the significance of patience and also shows its deep relationship with spiritual development and maturity.

When we face challenges and difficulties in life, it's natural to feel frustrated and overwhelmed.

However, true patience involves maintaining a sense of peace and trust in the midst of chaos. It's about surrendering to God's will and believing that everything happens for a reason, even if we don't understand it at the moment. By cultivating patience, we open ourselves up to a deeper relationship with the divine and allow ourselves to be guided by a higher purpose.

One key aspect of patience is the ability to let go of our need for immediate gratification and instant results. In a world that values speed and efficiency, patience shines as a beacon of perseverance and steadfastness. It teaches us to embrace the journey rather than fixate on the destination, recognizing that growth and transformation often occur in the waiting.

Moreover, patience fosters humility and empathy, as it requires us to consider the needs and feelings of others. By practicing patience, we learn to listen more attentively, forgive more readily, and love more unconditionally. It's a virtue that not only strengthens our relationship with God but also deepens our connections with those around us and yields enormous productivity.

In essence, patience is a spiritual discipline that invites us to navigate life with grace and wisdom. It teaches us to lean on our faith during times of uncertainty and to find peace in the midst of chaos. As we embrace the lessons that patience offers, we grow in resilience, compassion, and understanding. Ultimately, patience is not just about waiting; it's about trusting in the divine timing and surrendering to the infinite wisdom of God's plan.

Patience vs passivity
Patience is about waiting for the right moment while actively working towards your goals, knowing that good things take time. It involves persistence, resilience, and a steadfast belief in your plan, even when faced with obstacles. On the other hand, passivity is a state of inaction, where one lets circumstances dictate the outcome without taking any steps to influence it.

When it comes to financial planning, patience can be your best friend. It allows you to ride out market fluctuations and make informed decisions without being swayed by short-term trends. However, being patient doesn't mean sitting back and being idle as said earlier. It means staying proactive by setting clear financial goals, creating a budget, saving consistently, and investing wisely.

In financial planning, passivity can lead to missed opportunities and unnecessary risks. By taking a passive approach, you may neglect important aspects of your financial health, such as emergency savings, retirement planning, and debt management. Without proactive steps, you may find yourself unprepared for unexpected expenses or unable to achieve your long-term financial goals.

By combining patience with proactive financial planning, you can set yourself up for success. Start by outlining your financial goals and breaking them down into manageable steps. Create a budget that aligns with your objectives and use it as a roadmap to guide your spending and saving habits. Stay on course by regularly assessing your progress and making necessary adjustments.

Remember, financial planning is not a set-it-and-forget-it task. It requires ongoing attention and regular check-ins to ensure that you are on course to meet your goals. Stay informed about financial trends and seek advice from professionals when needed to make informed decisions.

Ultimately, patience and proactive financial planning go hand in hand. By staying patient and committed to your goals while taking responsible actions, you can build a strong financial foundation for the future. So, embrace patience, stay proactive, and watch your financial dreams become a reality.

Patience is indeed a virtue, but it's easier said than done, especially when anxiety, comparison, and discouragement pop up to test our resolve.

Picture this: You're feeling anxious, your mind is racing, and you're impatient for things to turn around. Pause, take a deep breath, and remember the wise words of Philippians 4:6 from the Bible, which says, "Do not be anxious about anything, but in everything by prayer and supplication with thanksgiving let your requests be made known to God." I believe that the 'anything' in that verse also entails money, fame, power and the likes. This encourages us to surrender our worries to a higher power, finding solace in prayer and gratitude.

When comparison creeps in, whispering doubts about your progress compared to others, remember this: Comparison is the thief of joy. Shift your focus back to your journey. Define your own path, set your own pace, and celebrate your unique progress. Remember 1 Thessalonians 5:11, "Therefore encourage one another and build one another up, just as you are doing." Embrace the idea of collective growth and support, rather than competing against one another.

Discouragement often sneaks in when things don't go as planned or the road ahead seems daunting. Turn to Romans 12:12 for a dose of encouragement,

"Rejoice in hope, be patient in tribulation, be constant in prayer." Keep the faith, find strength in hope, and maintain a consistent practice of gratitude and prayer during challenging times.

Financial challenges can actually be blessings in disguise—opportunities for spiritual growth, character development, and learning to lean on God. When we face money troubles, it's easy to feel overwhelmed and defeated. But let me tell you, that struggle can be a powerful tool for transforming our inner selves. It pushes us to dig deep, discover our inner strength, and build unwavering faith.

Think about it: when money flows smoothly, we might forget to appreciate the little things or take risks to grow. But when times get tough financially, that's when our resilience shines through. We learn patience, perseverance, and gratitude. We have a chance to strengthen our relationship with God, trusting that He will provide and guide us through the storm.

Next time you're facing financial hurdles, remember—it's an opportunity to unlock your true potential, nurture your soul, and deepen your faith. Embrace the challenge and watch yourself grow in ways you never imagined.

Trust in God for financial blessings and be filled with hope and faith. One essential way to cultivate trust is through prayer. In Luke 11:9-10, Jesus encourages us to ask, seek, and knock, assuring us that we will receive, find, and have doors opened for us. So, communicate with God regularly through prayer, pour out your heart to Him, and trust that He hears you.

Studying Scripture is another powerful tool. The Bible is filled with promises of provision and blessings for those who trust in God. Philippians 4:19 emphasizes that God will fulfill all of our needs based on His abundance in glory. Dive into the Word, meditate on passages that speak about God's faithfulness, and let these promises strengthen your trust in Him.

Surrounding yourself with supportive communities can also help in exercising your trust in God. Proverbs 27:17 (NIV) says, "As iron sharpens iron, so one person sharpens another." Being part of a community of believers can provide encouragement, guidance, and prayers that uplift you during challenging times. Share your journey of trusting God with others, and together, you can strengthen each other's faith.

When facing financial struggles or waiting on God for blessings, it's important to remember Psalm 37:7 (NIV), "Be still before the Lord and wait patiently for him..." This verse reminds us to trust in God's timing and to have a peaceful heart while waiting.

During problematic moments of doubt, fear and uncertainty, it's common to feel overwhelmed and unsure of the path forward. These challenging times can often leave you feeling lost and searching for guidance or reassurance, just remember Isaiah 41:10 (NIV), "So do not fear, for I am with you; do not be dismayed, for I am your God. I will strengthen you and help you; I will uphold you with my righteous right hand." God's presence provides comfort and strength, assuring us that we are not alone in our journey towards financial blessings. Sometimes, our impatience can hinder the blessings God has in store for us, so take a deep breath, be patient, and trust that God is working behind the scenes.

As you navigate the path of trusting in God for financial blessings, hold on to the promise in Jeremiah 29:11, "For I know the plans I have for you, declares the Lord, plans to prosper you and not to harm you, plans to give you hope and a future." Trust that God has good plans for you and wishes to abundantly bless you.

When anxiety strikes, try grounding techniques like taking a walk, practicing mindfulness, or journaling your thoughts. These activities help center your mind and bring much-needed calmness. Combat negative thoughts by reframing them positively. Instead of "I can't do this," say "I'm learning and growing every day." Focus on gratitude by keeping a gratitude journal, listing things you're thankful for each day. This practice shifts your focus from what's lacking to what you have, fostering patience and contentment.

Remember, patience is not about waiting passively but about having the strength to endure challenges and grow through them. Stay strong, stay patient, and remember that you're capable of navigating through any storm that comes your way.

As you embark on this journey of trust solely on God for financial blessings, remember to pray without ceasing, immerse yourself in God's Word, lean on a supportive community, and wait patiently with a peaceful heart. Have faith that God intends good things for you and wishes to shower you with abundant blessings.

Chapter 10
Avoid Greed: Do Not Chase After Wealth"

"Those who want to get rich fall into temptation and a trap and into many foolish and harmful desires that plunge people into ruin and destruction."
– 1 Timothy 6:9 (NIV)

In a universe filled with unlimited possibilities and alluring riches, the siren call of greed can be all-consuming. Everyone is striving to accumulate more, becoming fixated on wealth, possessions, or status making it easy to fall into the trap of always wanting what others have, comparing ourselves to them, and losing sight of what truly matters in life. Amidst these, we should consider drawing wisdom from the ancient book.

Greed, as defined by the Scriptures, particularly Proverbs 28:20 (NIV), "A faithful person will be richly blessed, but one eager to get rich will not go unpunished" serves as a warning against the dangers of an insatiable desire for material possessions or wealth. This verse highlights how those who are eager to get rich quickly will not go unpunished, indicating the consequences of allowing greed to take over. Greed is not just about wanting more; it is about an unreasonable and uncontrolled pursuit of wealth, power, or status.

The insidious nature of greed lies in its ability to constantly demand more without offering any lasting satisfaction. It thrives on the illusion that acquiring more possessions or wealth will bring happiness and contentment. However, as the saying goes, "The eyes of man are never satisfied." Greed creates a vicious cycle where no amount of wealth or possessions can ever satisfy its endless appetite.It is an endless and bottomless pit that can never be filled or satisfied.

The negative consequences of greed can be staggering, affecting both individuals and society as a whole. In Luke 12:15 (ESV), it is stated, "...Take care, and be on your guard against all covetousness, for one's life does not consist in the abundance of his possessions." This verse emphasizes the emptiness of pursuing material possessions as the sole source of fulfillment. When individuals are consumed by greed, they often prioritize their own desires above everything else, including relationships, ethics, and moral values.

On an individual level, greed can lead to a distorted sense of priorities. Instead of focusing on personal growth, relationships, or contributing to society, individuals consumed by greed become fixated on accumulating wealth or possessions. This singular focus can result in neglecting important aspects of life, such as personal well-being, spiritual fulfillment, and meaningful connections with others.

Society at large also bears the brunt of unchecked greed. When greed becomes pervasive, it fosters a culture of competition, distrust, and selfishness. The relentless pursuit of wealth at any cost can lead to unethical behavior, corruption, and exploitation of others. Such a society becomes divided, with disparities in wealth and power widening as a result of greed-driven actions.

Moreover, greed has a ripple effect that extends beyond the individual and societal level. It can lead to environmental degradation, as the relentless pursuit of profit often comes at the expense of natural resources and sustainable practices. Greed can also contribute to economic instability, as speculative behaviors driven by greed can lead to financial crises and market volatility.

Greed is a destructive force that can wreak havoc on both individuals and society. It undermines values such as compassion, generosity, and empathy, replacing them with selfishness, materialism, and discontent. The pursuit of wealth and possessions should be tempered with wisdom, humility, and a recognition of the true sources of fulfillment in life.

Wealth is often equated with material possessions and financial abundance in our society. But let's take a moment to dive deeper into the true essence of wealth.

Think about it – does true wealth really revolve solely around what we own or how much money we have in the bank? Maybe not. I believe wealth can also be found in inner peace, in the tranquility of our own minds and hearts. It's that sense of contentment that comes from within, regardless of external circumstances. When we can find peace within ourselves, we are truly rich.

And what about meaningful relationships? Think of the people in your life who bring you joy, love, and support. Those connections are like treasures that money can't buy. Building and nurturing these relationships can bring a richness to our lives that material possessions simply can't match.

Furthermore, true wealth lies in living a purposeful life aligned with our values. It's about knowing what matters most to us and living in a way that reflects those values. When we are living authentically and in alignment with our beliefs, we experience a deep sense of fulfillment that no amount of money can provide.

Take a moment to reflect on what true wealth means to you. Is it about financial success, or perhaps it's the joy found in meaningful relationships and experiences? Your definition of wealth is unique to you, so embrace it fully.

True wealth goes beyond dollars and cents; it encompasses fulfillment, purpose, and a sense of inner peace. It's the richness found in authenticity and personal growth. By defining your own version of wealth, you empower yourself to chase after what truly matters to you.

Strive to cultivate abundance in all aspects of your life—be it in your career, your relationships, or your personal pursuits. Your journey to true wealth is a testament to your commitment to living a fulfilling and purpose-driven life.

As you embark on this quest, remember that wealth is not just about what you have but who you are becoming. Embrace the journey, celebrate your milestones, and keep pushing towards your vision of true wealth. You deserve to live a life that is truly rich in all the ways that matter most to you.

Imagine a life where you wake up each day feeling a deep sense of peace, surrounded by loved ones who lift you up and support you. Picture yourself pursuing meaningful goals and living in a way that brings you fulfillment and aligns with your values. That, actually, is true wealth.

However, the journey to avoiding greed is full of challenges. One of the biggest obstacles is the societal pressure to constantly consume and acquire more. Advertisements everywhere lure us with promises of happiness through material possessions, leading us to believe that our worth is tied to what we own.

Moreover, our own desires and insecurities can fuel our greed. We may fear scarcity or feel the need to keep up appearances, leading us to seek fulfillment in possessions rather than in deeper, more meaningful aspects of life.

In the face of these challenges, it's important to seek guidance and wisdom. Proverbs 23:4-5 warns against laboring to be rich, for wealth can disappear in an instant. Instead, it encourages us to set our eyes on things that truly matter, things that last beyond material wealth. This scripture reminds us of the fleeting nature of material possessions and the importance of focusing on what is truly valuable.

As you navigate the journey to avoiding greed, keep Proverbs 23:4-5 close to your heart. Remember that true wealth lies not in what we possess but in the richness of our relationships, the kindness we show others, and the values we uphold. Stay grounded in what truly matters, and let go of the allure of material possessions that can never truly satisfy.

Ultimately, the path to avoiding greed is a journey of self-reflection, gratitude, and contentment. By cultivating a mindset of abundance and focusing on what truly brings joy and fulfillment, you can overcome the challenges of greed and lead a more satisfying and meaningful life. Let wisdom guide you, and may your heart be filled with the true riches that come from within.

Furthermore, let's explore practical ways to overcome greed using timeless wisdom from the Bible.

One powerful method is to cultivate a spirit of generosity. In Luke 6:38 (NIV), it says, "Give, and it will be given to you. A good measure, pressed down, shaken together and running over, will be poured into your lap. For with the measure you use, it will be measured to you." This verse emphasizes the principle that when we give to others without expecting anything in return, we open ourselves up to receiving blessings in abundance.

Another important step is to avoid the trap of comparison, as it often leads to feelings of inadequacy and contributes to a mindset of greed. The Bible warns us about the pitfalls of comparison in 2 Corinthians 10:12 (ESV), stating, "But when they measure themselves by one another and compare themselves with one another, they are without understanding." Focus on valuing your current blessings rather than measuring yourself against others, as pointed out in Hebrews 13:5 (NIV): "Keep your lives free from the love of money and be content with what you have, because God has said,OP 'Never will I leave you; never will I forsake you.'"

Developing healthy financial habits is crucial in overcoming greed. Proverbs 21:5 (New International Version) advises, "The plans of the diligent lead to profit as surely as haste leads to poverty." By setting clear financial goals, creating a budget, and practicing self-discipline in spending, you can avoid being consumed by the desire for more wealth. Additionally, seeking wise counsel on financial matters is wise, as stated in Proverbs 15:22 (NIV): "Plans fail for lack of counsel, but with many advisers, they succeed."

Moreover, understanding the transient nature of material possessions can help shift your focus away from greed. Jesus himself reminds us in Matthew

6:19-21 (NIV), "Do not store up for yourselves treasures on earth, where moths and vermin destroy, and where thieves break in and steal. But store up for yourselves treasures in heaven, where moths and vermin do not destroy, and where thieves do not break in and steal. For where your treasure is, there your heart will be also." By prioritizing eternal values over temporary possessions, you can find true fulfillment and contentment.

Remember, overcoming greed is a journey that requires intentionality and a shift in mindset. By practicing generosity, avoiding comparison, developing healthy financial habits, and focusing on eternal treasures, you can free yourself from the grasp of greed and live a more fulfilling and purposeful life. As you embark on this transformative journey, may these timeless truths from the Bible guide and inspire you.

Chapter 11
Be Honest in Financial Dealings: Integrity in Money Matters

"The Lord detests dishonest scales, but accurate weights find favor with him."
– Proverbs 11:1 (NIV)

Money — it's a funny thing, isn't it? It holds immense power over our lives, guiding our decisions, shaping our aspirations, and influencing our relationships. Think about it – from the moment we wake up to the time we go to bed, money creeps into almost every aspect of our existence. It dictates what we eat, where we live, how we dress, and even the opportunities we can grasp.

Financial dealings are like the threads weaving through the fabric of our lives, connecting us to one another and to the world at large. With money, we can create possibilities and unlock doors that were once firmly shut. It's the fuel that drives our ambitions and the lubricant that smooths the rough edges of our transactions.

But let's not sugarcoat it: money is a fickle companion. Just when you think you've got a grip on your finances, life throws you a curveball – unexpected expenses, fluctuating markets, job instability. Suddenly, what seemed like a sturdy financial plan feels as fragile as a house of cards. The complexities surrounding money can be overwhelming and sometimes even paralyzing.

Yet, amidst this swirling sea of uncertainty, one thing remains clear: the way we handle our finances can deeply impact our present and future selves. It's not just about accumulating wealth; it's about building security, fostering growth, and creating a legacy that transcends generations.

Whether we like it or not, money is a language we all must learn to speak. It's not just about dollars and cents; it's about understanding the value of our hard work, the power of our choices, and the importance of financial literacy. By equipping ourselves with knowledge and tools to navigate the murky waters of personal finance, we empower ourselves to make informed decisions and chart a course towards financial freedom.

I understand you may be thinking, "Money seems complex and complicated! Where do I even start from?" Trust me, you're not alone in feeling overwhelmed by the jargon-filled world of finance. Terms like stocks, bonds, dividends, and interest rates can make your head spin faster than a rollercoaster ride. But here's the thing: you don't have to be a Wall Street whiz to understand the basics of managing your money effectively.

Start small. Take a deep breath and dive into the world of budgeting. Think of it as your financial roadmap, guiding you towards your goals and helping you steer clear of financial pitfalls. Track your income, monitor your expenses, and identify areas where you can save or invest. It's like putting together a puzzle – each piece (or dollar) matters and contributes to the bigger picture of your financial well-being.

Always remember that it is perfectly fine to ask for assistance and seek help as you move on. Financial advisors, online resources, and even friends and family can offer valuable insights and guidance as you navigate the twists and turns of personal finance. Don't be afraid to ask questions, seek clarification, and learn from your mistakes. After all, nobody expects you to have all the answers right off the bat.

In the end, the true measure of wealth lies not in the size of your bank account but in the depth of your financial understanding and the resilience of your financial habits.

When it comes to financial practices, the Bible emphasizes fairness and justice. In Deuteronomy 25:13-16, there's a strong message about the importance of honest dealings. It instructs people to have accurate and fair weights and measures because cheating in these areas is seen as an abomination to the Lord. This emphasis on honesty ensures that everyone is treated fairly in financial transactions, promoting a just society where no one is taken advantage of.

Let's delve into the life of two biblical figures who exemplified wise financial management and learn valuable lessons from their experiences. Take Joseph, for example, whose story is told in Genesis 41:39-41. Joseph was put in charge of managing Egypt's resources during a time of plenty, and he implemented a strategy to save food during the abundant years to prepare for the upcoming famine. This foresight and responsible financial planning not only saved Egypt from starvation but also showcased the importance of wise financial stewardship.

Another figure worth mentioning is Zacchaeus from Luke 19:8. Zacchaeus was a tax collector known for his dishonest ways. However, after encountering Jesus, he repented and pledged to repay anyone he had cheated four times the amount. This act of restitution and accountability demonstrates the transformative power of honest financial practices and the importance of making amends for past wrongs.

These stories serve as powerful reminders of the impact of fair and just financial practices. They show us that honesty, transparency and integrity in our financial dealings not only benefit us individually but also contribute to a more equitable and just society as a whole. Just imagine if we all followed these examples in our financial decisions – the positive ripple effects would be immense.

Transparency in business is more than just a buzzword; it's about fostering trust and building strong relationships. Advocating for clear communication, accurate record-keeping, and avoiding misleading information in financial dealings is essential for maintaining integrity. When you cultivate transparency within your organization, you demonstrate that you value honesty and accountability. This, in turn, helps establish a sense of trust among your business partners, clients, and employers.

To foster trust and open communication, start by prioritizing honesty in all your interactions. Be upfront about any challenges or issues that may arise, and communicate openly with your stakeholders. This will create a culture of transparency that encourages others to do the same.

Additionally, make sure to listen actively to the concerns and feedback of your partners, clients, and employers. By showing that you value their input, you can build stronger and more meaningful relationships.

Another important aspect of fostering trust is to be consistent in your actions. Make sure that your words align with your deeds, and always follow through on your commitments. This helps establish credibility and reliability in the eyes of your business partners, clients, and employers. Moreover, when you make a mistake, own up to it and take steps to rectify the situation. This demonstrates integrity and shows that you are willing to learn and grow from your experiences.

One way you can build up honesty in your financial dealings is by focusing on ethical spending. This means being intentional about where your money goes. It involves creating a spending plan that reflects your values and beliefs. You can start by setting up a responsible budget that considers your income, expenses, and savings goals. This will keep you on track and help you avoid unnecessary debt that can compromise your financial integrity. When making purchasing decisions, prioritize ethical consumption choices that align with your principles, such as supporting sustainable and socially responsible businesses.

Avoid falling into the trap of impulsive purchases that can lead you away from your financial goals. Instead, take a moment to reflect on whether a purchase truly aligns with your values and budget. By embracing ethical spending, you not only make a positive impact on the world around you but also cultivate a sense of integrity in your money matters.

1 Timothy 6:10 (NIV), says, "For the love of money is a root of all kinds of evil. Some people, eager for money, have wandered from the faith and pierced themselves with many griefs." This directs us to the dangers of letting the pursuit of wealth lead us astray from what truly matters. By embracing ethical spending practices, you can avoid the pitfalls of greed and materialism, staying true to your values and faith.

Generosity is like the magic ingredient that makes life a little bit brighter for everyone involved. Just as I have earlier portrayed in the previous chapter of this book, when you choose to extend a helping hand or give back to those in need, you're not just making a difference in their lives—you're also opening up your heart to a world of positivity and abundance. By incorporating charitable giving into your financial plans, you're not just managing your money wisely; you're also investing in the kind of happiness and fulfillment that money can't buy.

Generosity in relation to showing and practicing integrity in money matters makes you open-handed and willing to help others without expecting anything in return. It involves being honest and fair in all financial dealings, even when no one is watching. By being generous with your resources and making ethical financial decisions, you demonstrate integrity by upholding your values and principles, regardless of the circumstances. Ultimately, generosity combined with integrity in money matters can lead to building trust and strong relationships based on honesty and goodwill.

Accountability can't be ruled out when expressing integrity especially in money matters. You know, having people around you who are all about doing the right thing and supporting you on your journey. It's like having your own little tribe of ethical superheroes! Why is this so important? Because we become the company we keep. When we're surrounded by folks who value the same things we do, it's easier to stay true to our own values and goals. Plus, these are the peeps who will give you that gentle push or nudge when you need it most.

So, finding mentors or accountability partners who get you and your values can be a game-changer. Imagine having someone who understands where you're coming from, who knows your dreams and aspirations, and who wants to see you succeed just as much as you do. That kind of support can be like rocket fuel for your journey. They can share their own experiences, offer guidance, and keep you focused when distractions try to pull you in different directions.

Think about it like this: when you're on a hike, having a buddy there to share the load and watch your back makes the journey a lot more enjoyable and less daunting. The same applies to your personal and professional development. Having ethical, supportive individuals by your side can make all the difference.

So, surround yourself with these ethical rockstars, seek out mentors or accountability partners who align with your values, and watch how your journey transforms. With the right people in your corner, there's no limit to what you can achieve.

Living with financial integrity brings so many wonderful benefits. When you manage your money wisely, you'll be amazed at the peace of mind it brings. No more worrying about bills or unforeseen expenses! Plus, it strengthens your relationships because you're not caught in the cycle of constantly worrying about money. You'll be able to be present and enjoy the moments with your loved ones. And let's not forget the deeper connection to your values.

When you align your financial decisions with what truly matters to you, you'll feel a sense of purpose and fulfillment that's truly priceless. So, stay committed to financial integrity, and watch how it transforms not just your finances, but your entire life for the better!

Chapter 12

Steward Resources: Manage Money as a Gift from God"

> *"Moreover, it is required of stewards that*
> *they be found faithful."*
> −1 Corinthians 4:2 (ESV)

Have you ever paused to ponder the countless blessings we enjoy each day? The air we breathe, the food on our tables, the roof over our heads—every single provision in our lives points back to the boundless grace of God. As we journey through the pages of our lives, it becomes increasingly evident that everything we have is a gift from above, a sacred trust placed in our care.

In the tapestry of our existence, one key thread we often overlook is money. Yes, money—a tool so ubiquitous in our daily lives yet so profound in its implications. But have you ever stopped to consider that money, too, is a gift entrusted to us by the Almighty? In the realm of stewardship, we are called not just to accumulate wealth but to manage it wisely, recognizing its divine origin and intended purpose.

As we delve into the realm of financial stewardship, one verse from the Good Book shines brightly with timeless wisdom: "In all thy ways acknowledge Him, and He shall direct thy paths." (Proverbs 3:6, KJV) This verse encapsulates the essence of stewardship—acknowledging God in all facets of our lives, including our finances, and trusting in His guidance as we navigate the winding paths of financial decision-making.

Imagine a world where each dollar earned, saved, or spent is seen as an opportunity to honor God—a world where financial blessings are viewed not as personal achievements but as sacred trusts to be managed with care and intentionality. This is the heart of financial stewardship: recognizing the source of our wealth, embracing the responsibility that comes with it, and seeking to align our financial choices with God's greater purposes.

As we embark on this journey of exploring the profound intersection of faith and finances, let us remember that every penny in our possession is a gift from above, a tool for good stewardship, and a pathway to deeper communion with our Creator.

The Bible talks a lot about the importance of being good stewards of our resources and being accountable to God for how we manage them. In 1 Peter 4:10 (NIV), it says, "Each of you should use whatever gift you have received to serve others, as faithful stewards of God's grace in its various forms." This verse highlights the importance of utilizing the talents and possessions we possess to assist and support others, understanding that all we own ultimately belongs to God.

Another powerful verse on stewardship can be found in Luke 16:10 (NIV), which states, "Whoever can be trusted with very little can also be trusted with much, and whoever is dishonest with very little will also be dishonest with much." This verse highlights the importance of being faithful and responsible with the resources, no matter how big or small, that God has entrusted to us.

When we apply these concepts to managing money, the message is clear: we are called to handle our finances wisely and responsibly, recognizing that we are merely stewards of the wealth that God has provided us. Our money and possessions are not truly ours—they ultimately belong to God. Therefore, we have a responsibility to manage them in a way that honors Him.

Being a good steward of your finances involves making wise decisions in how you earn, spend, save, and give our money. It means being intentional about budgeting, avoiding debt that we cannot repay, and being generous in sharing our resources with those in need. When we view our money as a gift from God and manage it with a spirit of accountability to Him, we can experience financial freedom and peace in knowing that we are honoring God with our resources.

One essential step about managing your money with wisdom and purpose and being a good steward of your finances is to develop a budget. Think of it as a roadmap that guides your spending in line with your values and priorities.

In creating a budget, start by outlining your income sources and all your expenses. This simple act helps you see where your money is coming from and where it's going. Transparency plays a crucial role in enabling you to make well-informed financial choices.

As you identify your expenses, take a moment to evaluate if your spending aligns with your values and priorities. Are you putting money towards things that truly matter to you? This introspection can lead to more mindful spending habits.

A fundamental principle mentioned in the Bible is found in Proverbs 21:5 (NIV), "Good planning and hard work lead to prosperity, but hasty shortcuts lead to poverty." This verse emphasizes the value of planning and diligence in managing your resources wisely.

By developing a spending plan that reflects your values and priorities, you're not only practicing good stewardship but also setting the stage for financial success. This approach can help you avoid unnecessary debt by being intentional about where your money goes.

Another powerful practice of managing money is mindful spending, it is a way of aligning your financial decisions with your core values. It's about understanding the distinction between what you truly need versus what you merely want. By embracing this mindset, you can sidestep impulse purchases and opt for intentional choices that enrich your life instead of draining your resources.

In the Bible, 1 Timothy 6:10 (NIV) warns, "For the love of money is a root of all kinds of evil." This verse highlights the importance of utilizing the talents and possessions we possess to assist and support others, understanding that all we own ultimately belongs to God.

Avoid falling into the trap of instant gratification with impulse purchases. Before buying something, ask yourself if it aligns with your true priorities and goals. Seek alternatives to expensive habits that may not serve your long-term well-being. Perhaps, consider DIY projects, swapping clothes or items with friends, or investing in experiences that bring lasting joy.

Remember, each dollar you spend reflects the type of world you wish to inhabit.. Be conscious of the impact your choices make, not just on your own life but also on the environment, society, and future generations. Choose to support businesses that share your values and contribute positively to the world.

By practicing mindful spending, you enrich your life with intention and purpose. You create space for what truly matters and ensure that your financial resources are a reflection of your deepest values. So, let your spending habits be a testament to your beliefs, generosity, and integrity.

May your journey towards conscious consumption be guided by wisdom and grace, as you cultivate a life of abundance that transcends material possessions. Embrace the power of mindful spending and witness how it transforms not just your finances but your entire existence.

Picture this: a life where you're not defined by the things you own, but by the experiences you've had and the values you hold dear. Imagine breaking free from societal pressures that push you towards materialism and instead focusing on what truly matters to you. It's about shifting your mindset from

"I need this to be happy" to "I value experiences and relationships over possessions."

When you step off the consumerism treadmill, you open up a world of possibilities. Think about the financial stability that comes with not constantly chasing the next big thing. Consider the deep fulfillment that arises from true connections and meaningful experiences, rather than temporary joy from buying something new.

And here's the kicker – when you choose to prioritize experiences and values over possessions, you're aligning yourself with a higher purpose. You're allowing yourself to connect more deeply with the blessings and rewards that come from wise stewardship. It's more than just about your bank account; it's about living a life that resonates with God's purpose for you.

Conclusively, remember that God entrusts us with resources not just for our own benefit but also to bless others and further His kingdom on this earth. By managing our money wisely and responsibly, we can fulfill our role as faithful stewards and live out our faith in a tangible way. Strive to be good stewards of all that you have been given, knowing that one day we all will be called to give an account of how we used the resources that God placed in our care.

Chapter 13
Plan for the Future: Secure Your Legacy

"A good person leaves an inheritance for their children's children, but a sinner's wealth is stored up for the righteous."
-Proverbs 13:22 (NIV)

This is a truth we all must face—the future is coming, whether we're ready or not. And deep down, we all want to leave a lasting legacy that goes beyond ourselves. We yearn to make a positive impact on our families, our communities, and the world at large. But how do we ensure that legacy reflects our values and intentions? The answer lies in one powerful tool: financial planning.

Think of financial planning as the blueprint for your legacy. Just like a builder wouldn't start constructing a house without a solid plan, we shouldn't navigate the future without a financial roadmap. In Luke 14:28-29, Jesus spoke about the importance of preparation, advising that no one begins construction without first calculating the cost to see if they have enough to finish. It's a clear call to make wise decisions and prepare for the future.

Proactive financial planning isn't just about crunching numbers and setting budgets. It's about aligning your resources with your values, dreams, and aspirations. It's about asking yourself: What kind of impact do I want to have? How can my financial choices today shape the world for tomorrow? By understanding the significance of every dollar, we can steer our resources towards what truly matters.

Imagine a ship without a captain or a map—lost at sea, tossed around by waves of uncertainty. That's what financial unpreparedness feels like. It leaves us vulnerable, reactive, and unable to navigate life's inevitable twists and turns. But with a solid financial plan in place, we stand firm against the storms of the future. We become the architects of our destiny, shaping a legacy that endures.

Take a close look at your financial landscape—your income, expenses, investments, and debts. Identify your long-term goals and set a course to achieve them. Seek wisdom in your choices, just as Proverbs 19:20 advises: "Listen to advice and accept instruction, that you may gain wisdom in the future."

Take a moment to envision the legacy you wish to leave behind. What values do you hold? How do you want to be remembered? By weaving these aspirations into your financial plan, you not only secure your legacy but also ensure that your impact reverberates far beyond your lifetime. Your legacy becomes a beacon of light, illuminating the path for future generations to follow.

In the fast-paced world we live in, it's easy to get caught up in the here and now, swept away by the urgent demands of today. But true foresight lies in the ability to see beyond the immediate horizon, to envision a future where your legacy stands tall, a testament to your vision and dedication. Ecclesiastes 7:12 reminds us that wisdom is a shelter, just as money is a shelter. But the advantage of knowledge is this: Wisdom preserves those who have it.

The future is not a distant realm to be feared but a canvas waiting for your brushstrokes. With faith as your foundation and wisdom as your cornerstone, embark on this voyage of financial planning with courage and conviction.

Securing your legacy is crucial. You need to start by developing a solid financial plan that covers all the bases. Think retirement savings, estate planning, and managing risks. This plan should be tailored to your unique circumstances and goals, so don't be afraid to get creative. Diving into the nitty-gritty of financial products is key. Explore options that align with your objectives. Whether it's investing in stocks, setting up a trust, or considering life insurance, there's a world of choices out there. And if all these terms start to feel overwhelming, don't sweat it. Seeking advice from a financial expert can offer valuable insights and peace of mind.

Saving for retirement is an important aspect of securing your future, and the earlier you start, the better. By beginning to contribute to your retirement accounts early on, you give your money more time to grow through compound interest. Consistency is key when it comes to saving for retirement—make it a habit to contribute regularly to your accounts to maximize your savings over time.

To calculate your retirement needs, consider factors such as your desired retirement age, estimated lifespan, monthly expenses, and potential healthcare costs. It's essential to be realistic about inflation and adjust your savings goals accordingly.

When choosing investment options for your retirement accounts, consider your risk tolerance and investment goals. Diversifying your portfolio can help spread out risk and potentially increase returns. Consult with a financial advisor to determine the right mix of assets for your retirement savings based on your individual circumstances.

Managing risks in your retirement savings involves adjusting your investment allocations as you get closer to retirement to reduce exposure to volatility. Consider gradually shifting to more conservative investments to protect your savings from market downturns as you approach your retirement age.

By prioritizing retirement savings, you are setting yourself up for a financially secure future. The key is to start early, contribute consistently, plan thoughtfully, choose suitable investments, and manage risks effectively.

It is crucial to protect your loved ones by planning for their financial security in case of unexpected events. Life insurance and disability insurance are key components in safeguarding your family's well-being. Life insurance provides a financial safety net for your loved ones in the event of your passing, ensuring they're taken care of in your absence. Disability insurance, on the other hand, provides protection in case you are unable to work due to a disability, ensuring that you continue to receive income to support your family.

When considering life insurance, there are various options available, including term life insurance and whole life insurance. Term life insurance provides coverage for a specific period, while whole life insurance offers lifelong coverage along with a cash value component that grows over time. It's essential to assess your needs and financial goals to determine which type of insurance aligns best with your circumstances.

In terms of disability insurance, it's important to look into policies that provide adequate coverage based on your occupation and income level. Disability insurance can help replace a portion of your income if you're unable to work due to an injury or illness. Considering the impact of lost income on your family's financial stability, having disability insurance can be a crucial piece of your overall protection plan.

As you navigate through these options, remember the guidance offered in Proverbs 27:12 (NIV): "The prudent see danger and take refuge, but the simple keep going and pay the penalty." This points us to the importance of preparing for the unforeseen and taking steps to protect ourselves and our families.

By exploring life insurance, disability insurance, and other financial strategies, you are demonstrating prudence and foresight in safeguarding your family's financial future. Making informed decisions about insurance coverage based on your unique circumstances is a proactive way to ensure that your loved ones are cared for in times of need.

So, take the time to review your insurance needs, seek guidance from financial advisors if needed, and make the necessary arrangements to protect your loved ones. By taking these steps, you are not only securing their financial well-being but also providing them with peace of mind knowing that they are cared for no matter what the future may hold. Remember, it is preferable to be ready than to be taken by surprise.

Planning your estate is another crucial step in securing your future. This ensures your hard-earned assets are distributed according to your wishes after you're no longer here. One key document in this process is a will. Think of your will as a roadmap that guides your loved ones on how to manage and distribute your assets. It gives you the power to decide who gets what, be it your savings, properties, or other possessions.

Having a will and other legal documents in place provides clarity and peace of mind. It helps you avoid potential family disputes and ensures that your assets are distributed as you intended. When navigating this process feels complex and a bit confusing, that's where seeking legal advice comes in handy.

Consulting with an estate planning attorney can help demystify the legal jargon and ensure your documents are properly drafted and legally binding. They can assist in structuring your estate plan effectively, considering factors like taxes, beneficiaries, and contingencies.

When preparing to create your will and other legal documents, gather essential information beforehand: details about your assets, debts, beneficiaries, and any specific wishes you have. This information will help streamline the legal process and make your intentions clear.

Now, let's talk about leaving a lasting impact. Incorporating charitable giving into your estate plan is a meaningful way to support causes you care about and create a positive effect beyond your lifetime. By including charitable donations in your will, you can leave a legacy that continues to make a difference in the world.

When considering impactful giving opportunities, reflect on causes that resonate with you personally. Whether it's supporting education, healthcare, environmental conservation, or any other cause, choose charities or organizations that align with your values and priorities.

Explore different ways to give back, such as setting up a charitable trust, endowment, or foundation. These structures can provide ongoing support to charitable causes and allow your philanthropic efforts to have a lasting impact.

In conclusion, estate planning is not just about managing assets but also about shaping your legacy and leaving a positive imprint on the world. By having a will and legal documents in place, you ensure your wishes are honored and your loved ones are taken care of. Consider incorporating charitable giving into your estate plan to make a difference in areas that matter to you. With proper guidance and thoughtful planning, you can leave a legacy that transcends generations and influences positive change in the world.

Planning for the future and securing a legacy isn't just about you—it's about leaving a mark that will positively impact generations to come. Paint a Picture of your great-grandchildren looking back with gratitude and admiration at the foresight and care you put into building a meaningful legacy for them.

By taking concrete steps now, you're not just ensuring your own financial security but setting up a strong foundation for your successors. Think of it as planting a tree whose shade you may never enjoy, but that will shelter many in the future. That's the power of planning ahead and creating a legacy that stands the test of time. It's always a good idea to start planning early, as it may become too late to do so at some point. Don't procrastinate when it comes to securing your legacy. Take the initial step today, regardless of how small it may look. Your actions now will have a positive lasting effect for generations to come.

Go ahead, take charge of your legacy, and watch as it blossoms into a testament of your foresight and love for those who matter most to you. Your future descendants will appreciate you for it. Start today, and pave the way for a legacy that truly matters.

Chapter 14

Be Vigilant: Guard Against Financial Temptations"

"Don't be obsessed with getting more material things. Be relaxed with what you have. Since God assured us, "I'll never let you down, never walk off and leave you,"."
– Hebrews 13:5 (MSG)

It's the end of a long workday, and you're scrolling through your favorite online store. You see that trendy gadget you've been eyeing for weeks, and without a second thought, you click 'Add to Cart.' Does this sound familiar? Oh yes! Trust me, we've all been there. The ease of online shopping, the lure of flashy advertisements, and the pressure to keep up with the latest trends can often lead you down the path of impulsive spending. You might end up making purchases without considering your budget or long-term financial goals. This temptation can derail your financial stability and put you at risk of overspending.

Then there's the pressure to keep up with others. You see your friends or colleagues flaunting their latest purchases or luxurious lifestyles on social media, and suddenly you feel the need to match up. This temptation can be driven by envy, greed or the desire to fit in due to the fact that our emotions often play a significant role in our financial decisions. pushing us to spend beyond our means just to maintain a certain image or status.

Get-rich-quick schemes are another common temptation. The promise of easy money or quick wealth can be incredibly enticing, but often, these schemes turn out to be too good to be true. Investing in risky ventures without proper research or understanding can lead to financial loss rather than gain. Greed plays a significant role here, clouding judgment and pushing individuals to take unnecessary risks.

And let's not forget about excessive debt. It's easy to fall into the trap of living beyond your means, relying on credit cards or loans to fund a lifestyle you can't afford. The burden of debt can weigh heavily on your financial well-being, leading to stress, anxiety, and a cycle of borrowing to make ends meet.

When it comes to the emotions of fear, greed, and envy influencing financial decisions, it's important to recognize how these feelings can impact your choices. Fear of missing out (FOMO) may drive impulsive spending or risky investments. Greed can blind you to the potential risks involved in certain financial decisions, leading to poor judgment. Envy, on the other hand, can fuel a desire to compete or compare with others, pushing you to make choices that may not be in your best interest financially.

In the Bible, 1 Timothy 6:10 (NIV) warns, "For the love of money is a root of all kinds of evil." This verse reminds us of the dangers of greed and the pursuit of wealth at any cost. It serves as a powerful reminder to prioritize values such as contentment, stewardship, and integrity in our financial decisions.

It is essential to cultivate self-awareness, set clear financial goals, practice discipline, stay vigilant and seek guidance when needed to navigate these challenges successfully.

Financial decisions are not just about numbers; they reflect our values, priorities, and beliefs. By staying mindful of the temptations and emotions that can sway us off course, we empower ourselves to make thoughtful, intentional choices that align with our long-term financial well-being.

At this moment you might be thinking, how do I stay vigilant against financial temptations? You need to:

Increase your knowledge: Learn budgeting, investing, and debt management basics.The foundation of financial resilience lies in creating a realistic budget that reflects your values and priorities. By setting clear goals and aligning your spending with these objectives, you can take control of your finances and make intentional choices that propel you towards your aspirations.

Identify your triggers: What emotions lead you to impulsive spending? Is it greed, envy, fear of missing out or the desire to fit in? Recognize them and create alternatives. By recognizing these emotional triggers and learning to control them, we can make more rational and informed choices when it comes to our finances.

Set goals and boundaries: When navigating financial temptations, setting clear goals and boundaries is your compass to stay on track. Start by defining your financial aspirations—whether it's saving for a dream vacation, buying a house, or building an emergency fund. Establish solid boundaries by outlining what you are willing and not willing to compromise on in terms of spending. Embrace the power of visualizing your goals to keep you motivated and focused when temptation knocks.

Track your spending: If you want to stay strong when financial temptations come your way, one smart move is tracking your spending. By keeping a close eye on where your money goes, you'll be more aware of your habits and better equipped to resist impulse purchases or unnecessary expenses. As the

Bible wisely says in Proverbs 27:23 (NIV), 'Be sure you know the condition of your flocks, give careful attention to your herds.' Just like a shepherd watches over their flock, you can watch over your finances through tracking, ensuring they stay healthy and flourishing. So, grab that budgeting app or notebook and start jotting down those expenses—it's a powerful way to outsmart those sneaky financial temptations.

Seek support: It is essential to recognize that staying vigilant to escape financial temptation can be challenging, so seeking support is crucial. Surround yourself with like-minded individuals who share your financial goals and values, whether it's family, friends, or a supportive community. Consider partnering with a financial advisor or mentor who can provide guidance and accountability. Additionally, take advantage of online resources, workshops, or support groups focused on financial well-being. Keep in mind that you don't have to go through this journey all by yourself. By building a strong support system, you can stay motivated, focused, and empowered to make positive financial choices aligned with your long-term goals.

Develop Healthy habits: You can build healthy financial habits that will help you steer clear of tempting spending urges smoothly. The secret sauce lies in mastering delayed gratification, where you resist impulsive purchases to achieve long-term goals. Focus on differentiating between needs and wants—prioritize the essentials, like bills and savings, over unnecessary splurges. Acknowledging what truly matters sets the stage for a stable financial future. Add the act of gratitude to your formula by appreciating what you have rather than fixating on what you don't. By being thankful for the present, you naturally curb the desire for fleeting indulgences. Remember, it's all about setting the right mindset and staying committed to your financial well-being.

Build strong defense: When it comes to staying vigilant and avoiding financial temptations, it's important to build strong defenses to safeguard your financial well-being. Some defenses include creating a spending plan that aligns with your income and goals, aims for 3-6 months of living expenses to buffer unexpected and emergency costs and managing debt by developing a plan to pay off debt and avoid accruing more.

By combining the practical strategies with biblical wisdom explained earlier in this chapter, you can build a solid defense against financial temptations and pave the way for a more secure and fulfilling financial future.

As you embark on your journey towards financial empowerment, remember that the path to success is built on a foundation of discipline, foresight, and resilience. By recognizing and resisting financial temptations, setting meaningful goals, and being intentional with your resources, you can pave the way for a future filled with prosperity and peace of mind.

Through the stories of those who have walked this path before you, let their experiences inspire and guide you in your own financial journey. Remember, you are capable of achieving greatness and securing a bright financial future for yourself and your loved ones. Stay focused, stay vigilant, and embrace the power of financial wisdom to transform your life.

Chapter 15
Practice Time Management: Utilize your time wisely.

"There is a time for everything,
and a season for every activity under the
heavens"
–Ecclesiastes 3:1 (NIV)

Time Management is a crucial skill when it comes to managing money effectively. Think about it; time is a valuable resource that, when utilized wisely, can have a significant impact on our financial well-being. When you manage your time efficiently, you provide yourself with the opportunity to focus on tasks that can directly impact your financial situation positively. Time management allows you to allocate your time wisely to activities that can help you earn more money, save diligently, invest wisely, and avoid unnecessary expenses.

Just like the popular saying goes, "time is money." The way you manage your time directly influences how you manage your money. If you can allocate your time effectively, you are more likely to make informed financial decisions, monitor your expenses diligently, invest prudently, and work on increasing your income streams. All these aspects play a crucial role in achieving financial stability and independence.

In the Bible, there is a verse that beautifully captures the essence of time management in relation to managing money. Ecclesiastes 3:1 states, "There is a time for everything, and a season for every activity under the heavens." This verse reminds us that time is a precious commodity given to us, and how we utilize it can significantly impact various aspects of our lives, including our finances.

When you manage your time effectively, you create the space to work on improving your financial situation. Whether it's allocating time to budgeting, learning about investments, working on a side hustle, or simply planning for the future, every aspect of financial management requires time and attention. By prioritizing your tasks and setting aside dedicated time for financial planning, you are taking a proactive approach towards achieving your monetary goals.

Moreover, effective time management can help you avoid impulsive financial decisions. By giving yourself the time to think through your choices, you are less likely to make hurried or emotional decisions that could have negative consequences on your finances. Time allows you to research, analyze, and evaluate different options before making a well-thought-out financial move.

Incorporating time management skills into your financial management strategy can also help you stay organized and focused. Setting clear goals, creating schedules, and establishing routines can streamline your financial tasks and ensure that you stay on track towards achieving your objectives. By managing your time efficiently, you can reduce stress, increase productivity, and ultimately enhance your financial well-being.

So, as you navigate your way through the realm of money management, remember that time is a valuable asset that can either work for you or against you. By mastering the art of time management and understanding its critical role in managing money, you empower yourself to make informed financial decisions, grow your wealth, and secure a stable financial future. Remember, as Ecclesiastes 3:1 reminds us, there is a right time for everything, including managing your time and money wisely.

Managing money wisely is not just about making a budget or saving a certain percentage of your income. It's also about setting priorities that align with your values and long-term goals. When it comes to prioritizing expenses, the Bible offers valuable wisdom in Matthew 6:21 (ESV), which says, "For where your treasure is, there your heart will be also."

This verse highlights the importance of aligning your financial decisions with your values and priorities. When you set your priorities right, you are more likely to make wise choices with your money. Think about what truly matters to you. Is it securing your future, helping others in need, or experiencing new things? Your spending habits should reflect these priorities.

Setting priorities in managing money involves making conscious decisions about where you allocate your financial resources. It's not just about cutting expenses but about directing your money toward the things that bring you the most value and fulfillment. This may mean sacrificing immediate gratification for long-term stability or investing in experiences over material possessions.

To effectively manage your finances, start by identifying your core values and long-term financial goals. Once you have a clear understanding of your priorities, create a budget that reflects these choices. Allocate your income based on what matters most to you, ensuring that your spending aligns with your values.

Prioritizing expenses also involves distinguishing between needs and wants. While it's essential to cover your basic needs such as food, shelter, and healthcare, not all expenses are equally important. Evaluate your spending habits regularly and identify areas where you can cut back on non-essential items. By focusing on what truly matters to you, you can allocate your time and money resources more intentionally and avoid wasteful spending on both.

Moreover, setting priorities in managing money empowers you to make informed financial decisions and stay on track with your goals. When unexpected expenses arise, having clear priorities helps you make swift choices without compromising your long-term objectives. By staying true to your values and goals, you can navigate financial challenges with confidence and resilience.

Absorb the wisdom of Matthew 6:21 and let your priorities guide your financial journey. Where you invest your treasure, there your heart will be also.

Eliminating time wasters is an essential step in effective time management. Wasting time is akin to squandering money. Just like you wouldn't want to squander your hard-earned money, you shouldn't squander your valuable time either. Time wasters can come in many forms - from aimlessly scrolling through social media to engaging in unproductive meetings or getting caught up in tasks that don't align with your goals.

Think about this Bible verse from Ephesians 5:15-16 (NIV), which says: "Be very careful, then, how you live—not as unwise but as wise, making the most of every opportunity because the days are evil." This verse stresses the importance of being wise with your time and seizing every opportunity that comes your way. Each moment matters, so we must be intentional with how we use our time.

To eliminate time wasters and boost productivity, start by assessing how you currently spend your time. Identify activities or habits that don't contribute meaningfully to your goals or overall well-being. Once you've pinpointed these time wasters, take proactive steps to minimize or eliminate them from your daily routine.

One practical way to do this is by setting clear priorities and establishing a schedule or daily routine that aligns with your goals. This could involve creating a to-do list or using time management tools to keep track of tasks and deadlines. By organizing your day effectively, you can limit distractions and stay focused on what truly matters.

Furthermore, understand the importance of refusing tasks or commitments that do not match your priorities. It's okay to decline non-essential requests or delegate tasks that can be handled by others. By setting boundaries and protecting your time, you can avoid spreading yourself too thin and ensure that your efforts are directed towards activities that yield the greatest rewards.

Additionally, practice mindfulness and avoid multitasking. Concentrate on a single task at a time, dedicating all your focus and energy to it.This not only helps improve your efficiency but also reduces the likelihood of making errors or needing to backtrack, ultimately saving you time in the long run.

Remember, time is a precious resource that should be valued and used wisely. By eliminating time wasters and increasing your productivity, you can make the most of each day, achieve your goals more effectively, and ultimately enhance both your time management and money management skills.
Take a cue from Ephesians 5:15-16 and approach your time with wisdom and intentionality. Make the most of every opportunity, eliminate those time wasters, and watch how your productivity and success soar to new heights.

Delegating tasks to others is a cogent step to managing time and money which is also a principle that is supported by the Bible. The art of delegating tasks is a true gem when it comes to making the most of your money. Imagine that you have a million things on your plate, bills to pay, investments to monitor, and perhaps even a side hustle you're trying to kick off. It can all feel overwhelming, right? Well, that's where delegating tasks steps in like a knight in shining armor, ready to save the day - or in this case, your finances.

Diving a little deeper into this concept with a sprinkle of biblical wisdom is the power of teamwork and delegation in Ecclesiastes 4:9-10 (NIV): "Two are better than one because they have a good return for their labor: If either of them falls down, one can help the other up. But pity anyone who falls and has no one to help them up." Oh, isn't that a beautiful reminder of the strength that arises from working together?

Now, imagine applying this principle to your financial management. By delegating tasks effectively, you're essentially creating a financial dream team around you. You might have a financial advisor to guide you through investments, a budget-savvy friend to keep you accountable, or even a virtual assistant to handle your administrative tasks. The key here is to recognize that you don't have to go at it alone - seeking help is not a sign of weakness, but a smart move in your journey towards financial prosperity.

Think about it this way: when you delegate tasks, you free up valuable time and mental space to focus on activities that truly add value to your financial well-being. Instead of getting bogged down with mundane tasks that eat up your time, you can channel your energy into strategies that boost your savings, grow your investments, and propel you closer to your money goals.

Delegate. That one word holds so much power when it comes to managing your finances wisely. It's like having a secret weapon in your arsenal, ready to streamline your financial workflow and elevate your money management game to new heights. So, don't hesitate to reach out for support, distribute tasks effectively, and watch as your financial journey transforms into a smoother, more efficient ride towards your goals. I would love to remind you that delegation is not just about passing off tasks – it's a strategic move that empowers you to make the most of your time and resources. As you embark on this journey towards wiser money management, embrace the concept of delegation with open arms. Build your financial dream team, share the load, and witness the magic unfold in your financial realm. With the power of delegation by your side, there's no limit to what you can achieve in your quest for financial prosperity. Goahead, delegate those tasks, and let your financial dreams take flight!

Another crucial step in effective time management to ensure financial stability and success is Strategic planning.. When we plan our tasks and budget our resources wisely, we set ourselves up for a more organized and fruitful life. Proverbs 21:5 (NIV) says, "The plans of the diligent lead to profit as surely as haste leads to poverty." This verse hammers the importance of diligence and planning in achieving financial prosperity. It highlights the contrast between carefully thought-out plans that yield positive outcomes and rushed decisions that can lead to financial ruin.

By taking the time to plan your expenses, investments, and savings, you can make informed decisions that align with your financial goals. Creating a budget, setting financial priorities, and regularly reviewing our financial status are all essential aspects of effective planning. Just as a builder needs a blueprint to construct a sturdy house, you need a financial plan to build a stable financial future.

When you plan ahead, you can anticipate potential financial challenges and take proactive measures to address them. Whether it's saving for emergencies, investing for the future, or paying off debts strategically, effective planning empowers you to make wise financial choices. As you cultivate the habit of planning and prioritizing your finances, you develop a sense of control and confidence in managing your money.

Remember, it's not about simply making a plan, but about diligently following through with it. Just as the verse from Proverbs highlights, diligence is key to reaping the benefits of our plans. Stay committed to your financial goals, adjust your plans as needed, and remain disciplined in your money management practices. With patience and perseverance, you can navigate financial challenges and strive towards a more secure financial future.

Strategically plan your finances thoughtfully and purposefully. Seek guidance from trusted sources, educate yourself on financial matters, and be proactive in managing your money. Let the wisdom of effective planning guide your financial decisions and lead you towards a prosperous and secure future.

Lastly, building resilience and adaptability in time and money management is crucial for navigating life's uncertainties, especially in financial dealings. Life can throw unexpected challenges our way, and being resilient and adaptable can help us bounce back and stay on track. In the book of Proverbs 24:27 (NIV), it is written, "Finish your outdoor work and get your fields ready; after that, build your house." This verse emphasizes the importance of planning ahead, prioritizing tasks, and being prepared for the future.

When it comes to financial dealings, building resilience involves creating a budget, saving for emergencies, and managing debt wisely. Prepare for unanticipated costs by establishing an emergency savings fund. This financial cushion can help you weather unexpected financial storms without derailing your long-term goals.

Adaptability in financial dealings is about being open to change and adjusting your strategies as needed. Just as a farmer adapts to changing weather conditions, be willing to pivot your financial decisions based on evolving circumstances. Whether it's adjusting your investment portfolio, finding new sources of income, or renegotiating expenses, being flexible can help you stay afloat during turbulent times.

Remember, setbacks are a part of life, but it's how you respond to them that defines your journey. Cultivate a mindset of resilience by staying positive, seeking support when needed, and learning from your experiences. Referring back to Proverbs 24:27, the verse encourages us to finish our work before building. This can be seen as a reminder to stay committed to our financial goals and persevere through challenges.

Building resilience and adaptability in time and money management requires planning, flexibility, and a positive mindset. By incorporating these qualities into your financial dealings, you can navigate uncertainties with confidence and emerge stronger on the other side. Stay focused on your long-term goals, be prepared for the unexpected, and remember that challenges are opportunities for growth. Just as a farmer tends to the fields before building a house, prioritize your financial foundation and watch it grow into a stable and resilient future.

In conclusion, time management plays a crucial role in shaping our financial habits and outcomes. By incorporating biblical principles and teachings into our approach to time management and money management, we can cultivate habits that lead to enhanced productivity, financial stability, and long-term success. Through setting priorities, planning effectively, seeking support, eliminating time wasters, investing in education, building resilience, and cultivating gratitude, we can align our time and resources with our values and goals, ultimately leading to a more fulfilling and prosperous life. As we continue to grow in wisdom and stewardship, may we seek to honor God with our time and finances, using them to bless others and make a positive impact in the world.

Conclusion

As we come to the conclusion of "The Divine Money Economics", I hope that the journey through these valuable insights has been enlightening and inspiring for you. Throughout this book, we have explored essential principles derived from the Bible that can guide you towards financial success and abundance in a way that honors both your spiritual values and your financial goals.

In exploration of assets and investment, you have learned the importance of being good stewards of the resources you have been blessed with. By understanding the value of what you possess and making wise investment choices, you can grow your wealth while also contributing positively to the world. Prioritizing giving reminds us that generosity is not only a virtue but also a key principle in attracting more abundance into our lives.

Avoiding debt and saving wisely are fundamental steps in achieving financial stability and freedom. By living within your means and cultivating the discipline to save for the future, you lay a solid foundation for your financial well-being. Investing diligently, seeking wise counsel, and working diligently are crucial components in building and safeguarding your wealth.

Practicing contentment encourages us to find joy and fulfillment in what we have rather than constantly seeking more. Contentment is a powerful antidote to the discontent that often leads to poor financial decisions and unhappiness. Being patient and avoiding greed explains that true wealth is not just about money but also about peace of mind and spiritual well-being.

Honesty in financial dealings is a non-negotiable principle that not only preserves our integrity but also fosters trust and respect in our relationships. As we steward our resources well, we acknowledge that everything we have ultimately belongs to a higher power – God, and we are called to use our resources in ways that align with our values and beliefs.

Planning for the future and being vigilant require foresight and discipline. By setting clear goals and being proactive in managing our finances, we can secure a brighter tomorrow for ourselves and our loved ones. Lastly, practicing time management underscores the importance of using our time wisely and efficiently, recognizing that time is a precious resource that should not be wasted.

As we reflect on these 15 timeless money management lessons from the Bible, let us not view them as mere suggestions but as practical wisdom to be applied in our daily lives. The central message of this book is clear: Financial Success is not just about amassing wealth but about living a life of purpose, integrity, and abundance in all areas.

Now, as you have journeyed through these lessons, I encourage you to take action. Apply the knowledge you have gained from these pages to transform your financial habits and mindset. Take a moment to assess your current financial situation and make a commitment to align your actions with the principles outlined in this book.

Remember, change begins with a single step. Start small, but start now. Whether it's creating a budget, setting financial goals, investing in yourself, or seeking guidance from a mentor, every action you take towards improving your financial well-being matters.

Believe in your ability to create the financial future you desire. Trust that by applying these timeless principles, you can achieve not only financial success but also peace of mind and fulfillment. Your journey to financial abundance begins with a decision and a commitment to take control of your financial destiny.

As you close the final pages of this book, let the wisdom you have gained guide you on your path to financial empowerment. May you walk with confidence, clarity, and purpose, knowing that you have the tools and insights necessary to create the life of abundance you deserve. May your financial success be a reflection of your commitment to living a life aligned with your deepest values and beliefs.

I sincerely appreciate and thank you for joining me on this transformative journey.
Wishing you prosperity, peace, and joy on your journey ahead.

Warm regards.

Index